Drafting and Negotiating Commercial Leases

Fourth edition
Supplement

Elizabeth McKibben Solicitor, Partner, Trowers & Hamlins
Dominic O'Neil Solicitor, Partner, Trowers & Hamlins

Foreword by **Murray Ross**, Solicitor

Butterworths
London, Dublin, Edinburgh
1996

United Kingdom	Butterworths a Division of Reed Elsevier (UK) Ltd, Halsbury House, 35 Chancery Lane, LONDON WC2A 1EL and 4 Hill Street, EDINBURGH EH2 3JZ
Australia	Butterworths, SYDNEY, MELBOURNE, BRISBANE, ADELAIDE, PERTH, CANBERRA and HOBART
Canada	Butterworths Canada Ltd, TORONTO and VANCOUVER
Ireland	Butterworth (Ireland) Ltd, DUBLIN
Malaysia	Malayan Law Journal Sdn Bhd, KUALA LUMPUR
New Zealand	Butterworths of New Zealand Ltd, WELLINGTON and AUCKLAND
Singapore	Reed Elsevier (Singapore) Pte Ltd, SINGAPORE
South Africa	Butterworths Publishers (Pty) Ltd, DURBAN
USA	Michie, CHARLOTTESVILLE, Virginia

© Reed Elsevier (UK) Ltd 1996

A CIP Catalogue record for this book is available from the British Library.

First edition	1980
Reprinted	1982
Second edition	1984
Reprinted (twice)	1985
Third edition	1989
Fourth edition	1994

ISBN 0 406 99314 9

Printed and bound in Great Britain by Ashford Colour Press, Gosport, Hampshire

Foreword

During the progression through Parliament of the Landlord and Tenant (Covenants) Bill in the autumn of last year it became clear that the Fourth Edition would require updating sooner than a new edition would permit.

I realised at once that pressure of work would make it impossible for me to undertake the task myself. I was delighted, therefore, when Elizabeth McKibben and Dominic O'Neil, Partners at Trowers & Hamlins, offered to step into the breach and undertake what turned out to be the huge task of producing a Supplement to the Fourth Edition. My intention with the book has always been to provide clear and succinct guidance for those engaged in the creation, sale or purchase of a lease; and the authors of the Supplement have fulfilled this objective magnificently, bringing the Fourth Edition fully up to date.

They have not only incorporated the new Act but much important case law; and the revision of the precedents will prove particularly valuable to all those grappling with the drafting of leases. I commend the Supplement to existing users of the book. I have no doubt that we will all benefit from the authors' very considerable efforts.

Murray Ross
July 1996

Preface

Since the fourth edition was published in March 1994 there have been some dramatic developments in the law governing the letting of commercial property. Most notably, the Landlord and Tenant (Covenants) Act 1995, hailed as the most significant piece of land law legislation since 1925, came into force on 1 January 1996. It abolished privity of contract for new leases and introduced a whole raft of measures to reduce the burden on former tenants and guarantors. One of the concessions offered to landlords, as the price of the abolition of privity, is the right for landlord and tenant to agree in advance the circumstances in which the landlord may withhold his consent to assignment and the conditions subject to which such consent may be granted. The Act is a complicated piece of legislation, with a number of flaws, and there is likely to be continued uncertainty about the effect of some of its provisions until the first cases on them are decided. In the meantime, a detailed understanding of the new law and careful drafting will be essential for landlord's and tenant's advisers alike.

In this supplement, therefore, we have endeavoured to bring the text of the fourth edition up to date to take account of the significant developments in this area of law. We have also included revised alienation clauses and an authorised guarantee agreement in the Precedents section.

But that is not all. In December 1995, the Department of the Environment published a new guide for the property industry, 'Commercial Property Leases in England and Wales—Code of Practice'. The Code is not prescriptive but the government will review its operation in a couple of years' time. Prior to that, in 1994, the Property Managers Association produced a guide to service charges in commercial leases. It remains to be seen how much influence the Code and Guide will have on practitioners.

There have been many important judicial decisions since the fourth edition. The decision in *Jervis v Harris* [1995] EGCS 177, CA has clarified the uncertainty surrounding 'enter, repair and charge' clauses and has substantially reduced the protection afforded to tenants by the Leasehold Property (Repairs) Act 1938. The House of Lords, in *Hindcastle Ltd v Barbara Attenborough Associates Ltd* [1996] EGCS 32, has made it clear that whilst the disclaimer of a lease will release the current tenant, it will not release his guarantor. This supplement also covers the latest developments in relation to VAT, environmental law in commercial property transactions, the CDM Regulations, 'keep open' covenants, the Disability Discrimination Act 1995, rent review and much more.

We are most grateful to Murray Ross for his considerable assistance in the preparation of this supplement. It has been a privilege to work with Murray and we thank him and others for their tremendous support.

We have tried to state the law as it stood on 1 January 1996 but have, where possible, included later developments where they have been of significance.

Elizabeth McKibbin
Dominic O'Neil
July 1996

Contents

Table of statutes

References in this Table to *Statutes* are to Halsbury's Statutes of England (Fourth Edition) showing the volume and page at which the annotated text of the Act may be found.
References in the right-hand column are to paragraph and page numbers. References in **bold** type indicate where the section of an Act is set out in part or in full. References in *italic* type refer to the pages of the Appendices.

Table of cases

F

G

H

I

J

Chapter 1

Drafting and negotiating leases

1.3

8   **Add:** The cautious draftsman should also avoid the 'torrential' style of drafting, for example including every potentially relevant word in an obligation without taking into account the fact that each may have a separate meaning and that taken together certain words may have cumulative meanings, see *Credit Suisse v Beegas Nominees Ltd* [1994] 4 All ER 803 (referred to at para 8.2 below).

1.5.3   **Add**: Fractions of a day are ignored.[7A]

7   **Add** to last sentence: and *Meadfield Properties Ltd v Secretary of State for the Environment* [1995] 3 EG 128.

Add: **7A**   *Bedding v McCarthy* [1994] 41 EG 151; *Supasnaps Ltd v Bailey* [1995] EGCS 89.

1.5.4

13   **Add**: *Trane (UK) Ltd v Provident Mutual Life Assurance* [1995] 3 EG 122.

1.6

1   **Add**: It is to be hoped too, that the lease does not omit a term agreed between the parties or include a term that had not been agreed: for a review of the principles for ordering rectification where this does occur, see *Brimican Investments Ltd v Blue Circle Heating Ltd* [1995] EGCS 18; *J J Huber (Investments) Ltd v Private DIY Co Ltd* [1995] EGCS 112.

Add: **1.6A**   Prompted by concern at the apparent imbalance in the position of landlords and tenants, the Department of the Environment published in December 1995 a new guide for the property industry, 'Commercial Property Leases in England and Wales – Code of Practice'.[1] Professional advisers[2] to both landlords and tenants are encouraged to draw the attention of their clients to the Code. Whilst it will provide no new insights for experienced landlords and tenants, the Code is geared towards small businesses and should prove to be a useful tool for solicitors in helping relatively inexperienced clients to understand the issues which are central to commercial lease negotiations.

1 (1995) RICS Book Department. The Code followed the Department of the Environment's consultation paper on the thorny issues of upward only rent reviews (see para 6.3 below), confidentiality and dispute resolution (see paras 12.6 to 12.8 below) and was introduced as an alternative to legislation. The Code is not prescriptive but the government has promised to review its operation after three years. Comments on the operation of the Code should be sent to the Code Secretariat at 12 Great George Street, Parliament Square, London SW1P 3AD. They will be considered by the Standing Committee set up to monitor the Code.

2 The Code was produced by (amongst others) the RICS, the Law Society, the ISVA, and the ABI.

Chapter 2

Non-drafting steps

2.5   **Delete** lines 6 – 11 (inclusive) and replace with: ... has confirmed by means of a certificate of lawfulness of existing use or development[1] or a certificate of lawfulness of proposed use or development[2] that the existing or proposed use or development is or will be lawful. With regard to the period during which enforcement action can be taken, the legislation provides that where a breach of planning control consists of the ...

In the fifteenth line **amend** the words 'in the change' to read 'of the change'.

1–3   **Delete** entirely and **replace** with:
  1 Town and Country Planning Act 1990, s 191.
  2 Ibid, s 192.
  3 Ibid, s 171B(1).

2.19

1   **Add:** The definition of 'tenancy' contained in the Landlord and Tenant (Covenants) Act 1995, s 28(1) includes an agreement for lease. This has a rather curious effect because s 3(1) of the 1995 Act provides that the benefit and burden of all landlord and tenant covenants contained in a tenancy shall be annexed and incidental to the premises. This extended meaning of tenancy means that any successor of the landlord or tenant would become liable to perform the obligations of the landlord or tenant under an agreement for lease (as well as the lease itself). In future, solicitors should check the terms of agreements for lease to see if they contain any outstanding obligations on the part of the party whose interest their client is acquiring. It is being suggested that landlords' solicitors should insert in leases a provision to the effect that the tenant can be required to confirm in writing to the landlord (or to any third party nominated by the landlord) that the only obligations of the landlord in relation to the tenancy are those contained in the lease. This is similar to the US practice where leases provide that tenants must give estoppel certificates when the freehold is being sold.

2.22–2.27   **Replace** section G   VAT, paragraphs 2.22 to 2.27.6 (inclusive) with:

G   VAT
2.22   *Background.* Value Added Tax ('VAT') is charged on the supply of goods and services in the United Kingdom when a taxable supply[1] is made by a taxable person[2] in the course or in furtherance of any business[3] carried on by him.[4] A taxable person is required to charge VAT on taxable supplies made by him[5] (output tax) and to pay this to HM Customs & Excise ('Customs') but before doing so he can deduct the VAT paid by him on goods and services supplied to him (input tax)

which relates to taxable supplies and account for only the balance.[6] If the input tax paid by a taxable person exceeds the output tax collected by him, he is entitled to a refund from Customs.[7] The supply of any goods and services will, for VAT purposes, fall within one of three categories: taxable at standard rate,[8] taxable but zero-rated[9] or exempt.[10] VAT is generally charged at the standard rate (currently 17.5%) but Schedule 8 to the Value Added Tax Act 1994 ('VATA') sets out 16 categories of goods and services that are zero-rated.[11] Thus the taxable person is not required to charge any VAT on them, but as they are taxable supplies, the principle of deducting input tax that is attributable to them still applies.[9] So a taxable person who supplies mainly zero-rated goods will collect little output tax. If the output tax that he does collect is less than the input tax that he pays, he is entitled to a refund of the difference.[7] Schedule 9 to VATA,[10] however, provides that other goods and services are exempt.[12] A business that supplies exempt goods and services cannot recover the input tax charged to it that is attributable to those exempt supplies. It has to absorb the VAT that it has paid, in the same way as the end (ie non-business) user, for example, in the form of increased rent or service charge.

Schedules 9 and 10 to VATA set out the main VAT rules relating to commercial property transactions.

1 VATA, s 5.
2 VATA, s 4(2), Sch 1.
3 VATA, s 94.
4 VATA, s 4(1).
5 Tax on any supply of goods and services is a liability of the person making the supply and becomes due at the time of the supply: VATA, s 1(2).
6 VATA, ss 24–26.
7 VATA, s 25(3).
8 VATA, s 2.
9 VATA, s 30.
10 VATA, s 31.
11 Including, for example, food, sewerage and water, books, newspapers, etc.
12 Including, for example, insurance, financial services, education, burial and cremation, etc.

2.23 *The new law.* Since the Finance Act 1989[1] (now consolidated in the VATA), VAT has been a factor in commercial conveyancing.[2] Now the only *zero-rated*[3] supplies are:

(a) the sale of the freehold or the grant[4] of a lease for a term certain exceeding 21 years by a person constructing a building designed as a dwelling[5] or a number of dwellings or intended for use solely for relevant residential[6] or relevant charitable purposes;[7]

(b) the sale of the freehold or the grant of a lease for a term certain exceeding 21 years by a person converting a non-residential building[8] or a non-residential part of a building into a building designed as a dwelling or number of dwellings or a building intended for use solely for a relevant residential purpose;

(c) work in the course of the construction of a building designed as a dwelling or number of dwellings or intended for use solely for relevant residential or relevant charitable purposes or any civil engineering work necessary for the development of a permanent park for residential caravans;[9]

(d)   work in the course of conversion by a registered housing association[10] of a non-residential building or a non-residential part of a building into a building or part of a building designed as a dwelling or number of dwellings or into a building or part of a building intended for use solely for a relevant residential purpose;[11]

(e)   the sale of the freehold or the grant of a lease for a term certain exceeding 21 years by a person substantially reconstructing a protected building;[12]

(f)   work in the course of an approved alteration of a protected building;[12] and

(g)   the supply of building materials by a supplier of construction work of the type mentioned above.[13]

The following are *standard rated*:[14]

(a)   the freehold sale of a partly completed building which is neither designed as a dwelling or number of dwellings nor intended for use solely for a relevant residential purpose or a relevant charitable purpose;[15]

(b)   the freehold sale of a new[16] building which is neither designed as a dwelling or number of dwellings nor intended for use solely for a relevant residential purpose or a relevant charitable purpose after the grant;[15]

(c)   the freehold sale of a partly completed civil engineering work;[15]

(d)   the freehold sale of a new civil engineering work;[15]

(e)   the provision of work to existing buildings (other than in the course of an approved alteration of a protected building);[17]

(f)   the grant of any interest, right or licence consisting of a right to take game or fish unless at the time of the grant the grantor grants to the grantee a fee simple of the land over which the right to take game or fish is exercisable;[18]

(g)   the provision in an hotel, inn, boarding house or similar establishment of sleeping accommodation or of accommodation in rooms which are provided in conjunction with sleeping accommodation or for the purpose of a supply of catering;[19]

(h)   the provision of holiday accommodation;[20]

(i)   the provision of seasonal pitches for caravans, and the grant of facilities at caravan parks to persons for whom such pitches are provided;[21]

(j)   the provision of pitches for tents or of camping facilities;[22]

(k)   the grant of facilities for parking a vehicle;[23]

(l)   the grant of any right to fell and remove standing timber;[24]

(m)   the grant of facilities for housing, or storage of, an aircraft or for mooring, or storage of, a ship, boat or other vessel;[25]

(n)   the grant of any right to occupy a box, seat or other accommodation at a sports ground, theatre, concert hall or other place of entertainment;[26]

(o)   the grant of facilities for playing any sport or participating in any physical recreation;[27] and

(p)   the grant of any right, including an equitable right, a right under an option or right of pre-emption, or in relation to land in Scotland a personal right, to call for or be granted an interest or right which would fall within any of paragraphs (a) to (o) above.[28]

The grant of any other interest in or right over land or any licence to occupy land continues to be *exempt* [29] but subject to one major qualification. Owners or landlords can elect on a property-by-property basis to waive the exemption and to charge VAT at the standard rate on the otherwise exempt rents and proceeds of sale.[30]

1 Section 18, and Sch 3.
2 VAT is a European Community tax and these changes were forced on the UK by a decision of the European Court of Justice in June 1988 (*EC Commission v United Kingdom* (1988) STC 456). The VAT system envisaged by European Community law does not provide for any supplies of goods or services to be zero-rated. As a transitional measure, member states where zero-rating was in force on 31 December 1975 were allowed to retain their zero-rating provisions until the advent of the Single European Market on 31 December 1992, provided the zero-rates in question were applied 'for clearly defined social reasons and for the benefit of the final consumer'. The Commission took the view that certain of the UK's zero-rating provisions did not comply with the condition and took proceedings in the Court of Justice to compel the UK to abolish them. The court *upheld* the Commission's view in the case of the construction and sale of commercial and industrial buildings; non-domestic supplies of water and sewerage services; news services other than those supplied to final consumers; non-domestic supplies of fuel and power; and protective boots and helmets supplied to employers for use by their employees. The court *rejected* the Commission's arguments on the construction and sale of new *domestic* buildings and the supply of animal feedstuffs, seeds and live animals for human consumption.
3 VATA, Sch 8, Group 5 and Group 6.
4 Grant includes assignment or surrender: VATA, Sch 8, Group 5, Note (1).
5 As to 'dwelling', see ibid, Note (2).
6 As to 'relevant residential purpose', see ibid, Note (4).
7 As to 'relevant charitable purpose', see ibid, Note (6).
8 As to 'non-residential building', see ibid, Notes (7) and (9).
9 See ibid, Item No 2, Note (19).
10 As to 'registered housing association', see ibid, Note (21).
11 Ibid, Item No 3.
12 See VATA, Sch 8, Group 6.
13 See VATA, Sch 8, Group 5, Item No 4.
14 Ie in most instances by virtue of being the exclusions from the exempt supplies set out in VATA, Sch 9, Group 1
15 Ibid, Item No 1.
16 As to 'new', see ibid, Notes (4) to (6).
17 Ie because such work is not zero-rated under VATA, Sch 8: see above.
18 VATA, Sch 9, Group 1, Item No 1(b).
19 Ibid, Item No 1(d).
20 Ibid, Item No 1(e).
21 Ibid, Item No 1(f).
22 Ibid, Item No 1(g).
23 Ibid, Item No 1(h).
24 Ibid, Item No 1(j).
25 Ibid, Item No 1(k).
26 Ibid, Item No 1(l).
27 Ibid, Item No 1(m).
28 Ibid, Item No 1(n).
29 Ibid, Item No 1, opening words. Prior to 1 March 1995, Note 1 of VATA, Sch 9, Group 1 stated that 'grant' included an assignment, other than an assignment of an interest made to the person to whom a surrender of the interest could be made. A surrender, or an assignment to the person to whom a surrender could be made, was thus regarded as liable to VAT. From 1 March 1995, 'grant' includes an assignment or surrender and the supply made by the person to whom an interest is surrendered where there is a reverse surrender. For these purposes, a 'reverse surrender' is one in which the person to whom the interest is surrendered is paid to accept the surrender. These changes to Group 1 were made following the

decision of the European Court of Justice in *Lubbock Fine & Co v C&E Comrs* (1994) STC 101. However, the effect of this decision in treating surrenders and reverse surrenders in the same way as other grants is retrospective, and therefore applies back to 1 April 1989 when surrenders became liable to VAT in the UK. In Business Brief 35/93 (20 December 1993) Customs invited tenants who surrendered their leases on or after 1 April 1989, and charged VAT, to apply for a repayment of the output tax. However, repayment will be denied where there would be 'unjust enrichment' of the tenant if a repayment were made. There will be no unjust enrichment where the payment was VAT inclusive as the tenant will have borne the VAT.

30 See para 2.25 below.

2.24 *Election to waive the exemption and opt to tax.* Apart from the specified exceptions,[1] the grant of any interest in or right over land, or any licence to occupy land, remains an exempt supply.[2] Schedule 10 to the VATA,[3] however, gives a person the right to elect that a particular grant will *not* be exempt, enabling him to charge VAT on rent or proceeds of sale ('opting to tax' or 'electing to waive the exemption', as it has come to be known) except[4] where:

(a) the building (or a part of it) is intended for use as a dwelling, or number of dwellings[5] or solely for a relevant residential purpose;

(b) the building (or part of it) is intended for use solely for a relevant charitable purpose, other than as an office;[6]

(c) the grant is made to a registered housing association and the association has given to the grantor a certificate stating that the land is to be used (after any necessary demolition work) for the construction of a building or buildings intended for use as a dwelling or number of dwellings or solely for a relevant residential purpose;[7] or

(d) the grant is made to an individual and the land is to be used for the construction, otherwise than in the course or furtherance of a business carried on by him, of a building intended for use by him as a dwelling.[8]

The election must be made on a property-by-property basis[9] and once made can be revoked (with Customs' written consent) within three months of its effective date, but not if either output tax has been charged or input tax has been recovered, or if the property has been sold during that time as a 'going concern'. The election can also be revoked after 20 years from its effective date, again with Customs' written consent.[10] The timing of the election is vital if all the input tax is to be recoverable.[11] The aim of the concept of opting to tax is to overcome the hardship that would apply if the grant of a lease or sale of a freehold was always an exempt supply. A person who had paid VAT and incurred input tax on, for example, the construction or purchase of a new commercial building and who then let it would be unable to recover any input tax if the rent (which was his only supply) was always exempt. The fact that he can waive this exemption gives him the opportunity to recover input tax.[12]

In certain circumstances Customs' permission is required before an election can be made.[13]

1 Ie those specified in VATA, Sch 9, Group 1, Item No 1(a)–(n).
2 Ibid, Item No 1.
3 Ibid, para 2(1).

4 These (and the supplies that are not exempt: see note 1 above) are the only exceptions. So the election to waive the exemption applies to all other properties, including (for example) new and old buildings, agricultural land.
5 VATA, Sch 10, para 2(2)(a).
6 Ibid, para 2(2)(b).
7 Ibid, paras 2(3)(a) and 3(8).
8 Ibid, para 2(3)(b).
9 Ibid, para 2(1). As to when an election is made in relation to part of a building see ibid, para 3(3).
10 Ibid, paras 3(4) and 3(5).
11 Ibid, paras 2(4),(5),(6),(7),and 3(1).
12 See para 2.22 above.
13 VATA Sch 10, para 3(9).

2.25 *VAT payable – who suffers?* A purchaser or tenant who is himself a taxable person supplying standard or zero-rated supplies will have no fundamental concern if the purchase price or rent of his property attracts VAT.[1] It will no doubt increase his input tax but as he can deduct this from his output tax and claim a refund if inputs exceed outputs, his only potential problem could be one of cashflow, having to fund the inputs before he has received outputs to set off against them or (where inputs exceed outputs) before he receives the refund at the end of the prescribed accounting period.[1] The purchasers or tenants who will suffer will be those who supply exempt services, for example banks, building societies, insurance companies and private schools. They will have nothing to set against the additional 17.5% payable on their rent and purchase price and will simply have to absorb this or pass it on as higher charges or fees. They are known as VAT-adverse tenants and purchasers.

1 See para 2.22 above. The only qualification to this statement is that he will have to pay stamp duty on the VAT as well as the purchase price: VATA, s 19(2).

2.26 *Practical issues.* The property lawyer must consider the VAT implications in a number of situations—for example:

2.26.1 *Property development.* VAT must be added to the list of factors that will need considering during the planning stage of any proposed commercial development by all the parties and their advisers.[1]

2.26.2 *Waiving exemption.* When a sale or lease of commercial premises is being contemplated that would otherwise produce exempt proceeds of sale or rents, the advisers to the potential vendor or landlord need to consider if their client should elect to waive the exemption so as to be able to charge VAT and thereby recover input tax.[2]

2.26.3 *Registered for VAT.* Where a party has not made taxable supplies before, he will need to be registered. A purchaser or tenant who wishes to set off the input tax paid by him against the output tax charged to him must also be registered.[3]

2.26.4 *Purchaser's and tenant's concerns.* A purchaser's or tenant's solicitor should always enquire of the vendor's or landlord's solicitor if the exemption has been waived.[4] A vendor who has not done so should be required in the contract to warrant that the exemption has not been waived and to covenant that it will not be waived after exchange of contracts. A tenant who supplies mainly goods and services that are exempt[5] should seek a covenant in the lease preventing the landlord from waiving the exemption at any time during the term of the lease.

2.26.5 *VAT invoice.* Whenever a person pays VAT, he should obtain a VAT invoice, otherwise his claim to set the input tax incurred on that supply against his output tax is at the discretion of Customs.[6]

2.26.6 *Drafting.* Whether or not the landlord has elected to waive the exemption, his solicitor must ensure that the lease contains a covenant by the tenant to pay to the landlord any VAT chargeable on the rent or on any payment made under the lease in addition to the rent.[7] If the lease is silent as to whether any VAT chargeable on the rent can be added to the rent, the position is as follows:

(a) the landlord *will* be able to add VAT where the lease is dated before 1 August 1989 whenever he opts to tax because there will have been a change in the rate of tax since the lease was made and VATA, s 89 will apply;

(b) he *will* be able to add VAT where the lease is dated on or after 1 August 1989 and where the option to tax is exercised after the date of the lease for the same reason; but

(c) he *will not* be able to add VAT where the lease is dated on or after 1 August 1989 but where the option to tax had been exercised before the date of the lease. Here VATA, s 89 will not apply, because there has been no change in the rate of tax since the lease was made, and the basic provision set out in VATA, s 19(2) will apply, to the effect that where a contract is silent, the presumption is that the price is *inclusive* of VAT. This does not prevent the landlord from opting to tax but it does mean that the tenant will continue to pay the same amount of rent but a proportion of it will be VAT – for every £1,000 of rent, the landlord will receive only £851.06,[8] the balance being VAT.

1 See para 2.25 above.
2 See para 2.24 above.
3 VATA, ss 24–26, Sch 1.
4 See para 2.24 above.
5 See para 2.22, notes 10 and 12 above.
6 VATA, s 24 and the Value Added Tax (General) Regulations 1995, regs 13 and 29.
7 See, for example, Appendix 1, Form 1.1, clause 10.3.
8 Assuming VAT of 17.5%.

Chapter 3

The parcels

3.19

4   **Add:** It is important for capital allowances purposes to establish which items are fixtures and who will be entitled to capital allowances on those items. Until 1984 only the landlord could claim capital allowances on fixtures because they did not 'belong' to the tenant (*Stokes v Costain Property Investments Ltd* (1984) 57 TC 688). However, the Finance Act 1985 changed the position by introducing new rules concerning entitlement to capital allowances on landlord's fixtures. The position now is that where a tenant incurs expenditure after 11 July 1984 on machinery or plant which becomes a fixture (for example, an air conditioning or central heating system), the machinery and plant is deemed to belong to the tenant for capital allowances purposes (s 52, Capital Allowances Act 1980 ('CAA')). There are no special provisions in the CAA as regards what is a fixture and therefore the ordinary land law applies; and if such an item is treated as belonging to a tenant for capital allowances purposes, no one else is entitled to an allowance in respect of it (s 51, CAA). Where, after any item of machinery or plant has become a fixture a purchaser acquires an existing interest in the land and part of the purchase price is attributable to the fixtures then, subject to certain conditions, the fixture is treated as belonging to the purchaser (s 54, CAA). This would cover, for example, the assignment of a lease. Also, when a landlord grants a new lease and the consideration given by the incoming tenant includes a capital sum for fixtures, subject to certain conditions, the tenant is entitled to capital allowances. It may be necessary for the landlord and tenant to make a joint election to this effect (ss 55 and 56, CAA). There are also special rules governing disposal values of fixtures for capital allowances purposes when a lease is assigned, surrendered or expires (ss 57 and 59, CAA 1990).

5   **Add:** In *TSB Bank plc v Botham* [1995] EGCS 3, carpets, light fittings, gas fires, curtains and blinds, towel rails and kitchen units were held to be fixtures but the decision has been much criticised. The more recent case of *Aircool Installations v British Telecom* [1995] 3 CLW 18/95, in which air-conditioning equipment was held to be a fixture, adopted a less controversial approach, in line with the recognised authorities.

Chapter 4

Rights, exceptions and reservations

4.2   **Add:**   In *CIN Properties Ltd v Rawlins*,[4] the Court of Appeal considered the circumstances in which members of the public could be excluded from a shopping centre. CIN had sought to exclude a group of individuals whose behaviour had been alleged to be a nuisance. The Court held that CIN was entitled to revoke the defendants' licences to enter the centre without need to show any cause. The Court rejected an argument that the pedestrian malls within the centre had been dedicated as a public highway and, on the facts of the case, dismissed the suggestion that a covenant by CIN, contained in its lease from the local authority, to allow pedestrian access to the common parts from 7.00am to 11.00pm daily, amounted to a walkways agreement.[5] The Court considered that the Highways Act 1980, s 35 made sufficient provision for dealing with shopping centres and refused to extend to this country the proposition, based on a dissenting opinion in the North American case of *Harrison v Carswell*,[6] that the owners of shopping centres should only be able to revoke a member of the public's licence to enter the centre upon misbehaviour or by reason of his unlawful activity.

Add: 4   [1995] 39 EG 148.
          5   At the time of the lease covered by the Highways Act 1971, s 18, but now the Highways Act 1980, s 35.
          6   (1975) 62 DLR (3d) 68, per Laskin CJC.

4.13

2   **Add**: See also *Meadows v Home Properties Ltd* [1993] EGCS 50.

Chapter 5

Before the covenants

5.3

Add: 1   See also *Ingram v IRC* [1995] STC 564 in which it was held, inter alia, that a lease involved the creation of mutual rights and obligations which could only be given any meaning if entered into between independent parties (and, thus, a nominee could not grant an effective lease to his principal). Whilst the Inland Revenue lodged an appeal against the decision in this case in November 1995, it would be surprising if this principle were undermined.

5.5   **Delete** the last sentence and **replace** with: In respect of those leases which are not 'new tenancies' for the purposes of the Landlord and Tenant (Covenants) Act 1995,[7] a landlord who obtained a good original tenant will also have acquired a guarantor for all assignees. The same will not be true of new tenancies since the 1995 Act has effectively abolished the continuing liability of original tenants which existed by virtue of the doctrine of privity of contract.[8] Nothing in the 1995 Act prevents a landlord from requiring contractual guarantors for either the original tenant or a subsequent assignee.[9] However, the liability of the guarantor under a new tenancy cannot last longer than that of the tenant or assignee which it guarantees.[10] Landlords' solicitors should ensure that the liability of the guarantor is expressed to last whilst the tenant or assignee is bound by the tenant's covenants contained in the lease,[11] rather than whilst the lease is vested in that person, in order to take account of the possibility of an excluded assignment [12] being made and the tenant or assignee remaining liable.[13]

7   **Delete** entirely and **replace** with: 7   For the distinction between new tenancies and old leases, see para 5.11 below.

Add: 8   See paras 5.11 to 5.15 below.

9   In respect of any proposed assignment, a landlord may require guarantors either when it is reasonable to do so under Landlord and Tenant Act 1927, s 19(1)(a) (23 *Halsbury's Statutes* (4th edn) LANDLORD AND TENANT) or because the provision of such guarantors is a condition inserted in a new tenancy under Landlord and Tenant Act 1927, s 19(1A) as inserted by Landlord and Tenant (Covenants) Act 1995, s 22 (23 *Halsbury's Statutes* (4th edn) LANDLORD AND TENANT), ie a condition regulating the giving of the landlord's consent to assignment (see para 7.5A below).

10   Landlord and Tenant (Covenants) Act 1995, s 24(2) (23 *Halsbury's Statutes* (4th edn) LANDLORD AND TENANT). Though see para 5.6.7 below.

11   See Appendix 1, Form 1.1, Clause 19.

12   Eg where the tenant assigns either in breach of covenant or by operation of law (eg on the death or bankruptcy of the tenant), Landlord and Tenant (Covenants) Act 1995, s 11. See para 5.13.1 below.

13   An excluded assignment means that the tenant is precluded from tenant release under the 1995 Act.

5.6.2

4   **Add**: *Howard de Walden Estates Ltd v Pasta Place Ltd* [1995] 22 EG 143; *West Horndon Industrial Park v Phoenix Timber* [1995] MPC 42, [1995] 20 EG 137; and *Metropolitan Properties Co Regis Ltd v Bartholomew* [1995] 14 EG 143 discussed at [1995] 40 EG 137.

5.6.4   Delete this paragraph and **replace** with:

Disclaimer.   Following the House of Lords decision in *Hindcastle v Barbara Attenborough Associates Ltd,*[9] unless the landlord takes possession a disclaimer of the lease by the tenant's liquidator or trustee in bankruptcy will not release the guarantor of that insolvent tenant (or the guarantor of any former tenant who continues to be liable). Although the lease itself will come to an end upon disclaimer, the liability of the guarantor will continue as though the lease were still in existence. The guarantor of the insolvent tenant may apply for an overriding lease under the provisions of the Landlord and Tenant (Covenants) Act 1995.[10] It is suggested that for the sake of clarity landlords continue to draft the guarantor's covenant so as to require the guarantor, in the event of a disclaimer, to accept a lease of the premises for the residue of the term which would have remained had there been no disclaimer.[10A]

9   **Delete** entirely.

10   **Renumber** as '10A'.

Add: 9   [1996] 2 WLR 262, overruling *Stacey v Hill* [1901] 1 KB 660.
          10   See para 5.14.2 below.

Add: **5.6.7** *Drafting considerations in the light of the 1995 Act.*[16] In the past, landlords were content to grant leases to tenants of nominal worth, such as weak subsidiaries, provided that substantial guarantors were furnished, such as the subsidiary's parent company. This practice could now lead to problems. As soon as the tenant is released by the 1995 Act then so too is its guarantor,[17] but only the former tenant can be required to enter into an authorised guarantee agreement upon assignment.[18] An authorised guarantee agreement entered into by a newly formed company or weak subsidiary may be virtually worthless. It is not clear from the 1995 Act whether the liability of a contractual guarantor can be expressed to extend to any period during which the tenant is bound by an authorised guarantee agreement. Some commentators believe that the policy of the 1995 Act suggests that this should be acceptable whereas others fear that any attempt to require the tenant's guarantor to enter into the authorised guarantee agreement, either directly or as guarantor of the tenant's liabilities, could be attacked as falling foul of the anti-avoidance provisions of the 1995 Act[19] in that it would be an attempt to modify the operation of the guarantor's release.[20] Until this point is clarified, guarantees could be drafted to make clear that the contractual guarantor is liable for three potential periods:

(a)   while the lease is vested in the tenant;
(b)   an extended period while the tenant is bound by the tenant's covenants contained in the lease; and

(c)   any period during which the tenant is liable under an authorised guarantee agreement.

If distinctly drafted, the periods ought to be severable should a court find that the third period is an unacceptable extension of liability. In practice landlords are reviewing their letting policy in relation to guarantors and now generally insist upon the financially sound party being the tenant (or a joint tenant) and not merely guarantor.

Add: 16   This paragraph relates only to new tenancies under the 1995 Act.
      17   See Landlord and Tenant (Covenants) Act 1995, s 24 (23 *Halsbury's Statutes* (4th edn) LANDLORD AND TENANT).
      18   See ibid, s 16. As to authorised guarantee agreements generally, see para 5.13.2 below.
      19   See ibid, s 25.
      20   See ibid, s 24. See also Steven Fogel and Emma Slessenger 'The Landlord and Tenant (Covenants) Act 1995: Where does it fall short of its presumed intent?' (The Blundell Memorial Lectures 1996).

5.7.2

3   **Delete** from 'is the guarantee ...' to '... in question, and' (inclusive).

5.8
(b)   **Add** after the word 'will' in the first line: ', in the case of old leases,[2A]'.

       Amend the words 'be agreeing' in the third line to 'have agreed'.

Add: 2A   See para 5.11 below.

(d)   **Add:** '[6A]' after the word 'problem' in the fourth line.

Add: 6A   However, in respect of old leases (see para 5.11 below), where a guarantor remains liable under his guarantee after the tenant has assigned his interest in the property, the guarantor will not be liable in respect of a covenant under which any fixed charge is payable unless the landlord serves notice upon him within six months of the date that the fixed charge becomes due (see Landlord and Tenant (Covenants) Act 1995, s 17(3), (23 *Halsbury's Statutes* (4th edn) LANDLORD AND TENANT). See also para 5.14.1 below.

5.9.1   **Delete** the sentence commencing 'Should this be...' and **replace** with: 'The guarantor should try to resist any attempt by the landlord to extend the guarantor's liability to cover any period during which the tenant is liable under an authorised guarantee agreement.[2]'

5.9.5   **Add:** Since the default notice provisions contained in the 1995 Act[4A] do not extend to guarantors,[4B] the guarantor might also insert in the lease an additional provision requiring the landlord to serve on the guarantor the equivalent of a default notice.[4C]

5.9.6   **Delete** (b) and **replace** with:

(b)   Where the guarantee is expressed to apply during any period in which the tenant is liable under an authorised guarantee agreement, there would have to be a provision dealing with the assignment, as the original tenant could hardly purport to appoint an attorney on behalf of his assignee.[6]

5.9.8 Delete the last sentence entirely.

2   **Delete** entirely and replace with: 2   See para 5.6.7 above.

Add: **4A**   See para 5.14.1 below.
       4B   1995 Act, s 17(3).
       4C   For a precedent see Butterworths' *Encyclopaedia of Forms and Precedents*, Volume 22 (Landlord and Tenant) (5th edn, Form 225.7.)

5.11– Replace section D ORIGINAL TENANT AS GUARANTOR,
5.14 paragraphs 5.11 to 5.14 (inclusive) with:

D. THE TENANT AS GUARANTOR

5.11 *The Landlord and Tenant (Covenants) Act 1995.* The 1995 Act came into force on 1 January 1996 and has been hailed as the most dramatic piece of landlord and tenant legislation for 40 years. For leases granted on or after that date,[1] the doctrine of privity of contract is effectively abolished and a new regime has been created governing the relationship between landlord and tenant. Since the 1995 Act is not retrospective, it is critical to distinguish between what may be termed 'old leases', in respect of which the original contracting parties[2] will continue to remain liable throughout the term of the lease, and 'new tenancies' which will be subject to the new regime. For the purposes of the 1995 Act a new tenancy is one granted on or after 1 January 1996 unless:

(a) the tenancy is preceded by an agreement for lease entered into before that date;[3]

(b) the tenancy is pursuant to a court order (eg under Part II of the 1954 Act) made before 1 January 1996;[4]

(c) the tenancy is pursuant to an option (including a right of first refusal) granted before 1 January 1996;[5] or

(d) the tenancy is an overriding lease where the original tenancy was an old lease.[6]

The 1995 Act preserves the rule that variations may operate as deemed surrenders and re-grants. Following a surrender and re-grant made on or after 1 January 1996, the lease will become a new tenancy.[7]

Apart from the transitional cases referred to at (a) and (b) above, leases renewed under the 1954 Act which are granted after 1 January 1996 will be new tenancies.[8]

1   But see the definition of a new tenancy below for those exceptional leases granted on or after 1 January 1996 which will still be subject to the old law of privity of contract.
2   And more often than not, in the case of tenants, subsequent assignees.
3   1995 Act, s 1(3)(a) (23 *Halsbury's Statutes* (4th edn) LANDLORD AND TENANT).
4   Ibid, s 1(3)(b).
5   Ibid, s 1(6),(7).
6   Ibid, ss 1(4) and 20(1). As to overriding leases see para 5.14.2 below.
7   Ibid, s 1(5).
8   1954 Act, s 35(2) as inserted by the 1995 Act, s 30(1), Sch 1, para 4 (23 *Halsbury's Statutes* (4th edn) LANDLORD AND TENANT), whereby the court is directed to take this change into account. Landlords will therefore be able to argue for a compensatory change to the assignment provisions in the lease, notwithstanding *O'May v City of London Real Property Co Ltd* [1983] 2 AC 726. See para 7.5A below for the right to agree in advance the terms on which consent to assign will be given.

5.12 *Old leases: The original tenant as guarantor.* In respect of old leases, which will continue to be subject to the doctrine of privity of contract, the original tenant[1] remains liable to the landlord[2] for any breach of the tenant's obligations[3] contained in the lease,[4] notwithstanding the fact that the tenant may have assigned the lease.[5] The landlord owes no duty to the original tenant properly to assess the creditworthiness of a subsequent assignee or to take proper and timely measures to enforce the covenants against the assignee before claiming from the original tenant.[6] Whether the liability extends to a statutory continuation under the 1954 Act will depend upon the wording of the lease.[7] The original tenant will no doubt have obtained an express or implied[8] covenant of indemnity in respect of a breach committed at any time[9] after it has assigned the lease[10] but this will be of no assistance to it if the assignee is insolvent.[11] Therefore the original tenant will have many of the concerns of a guarantor.[12] However, the position of former tenants and their guarantors under old leases has been significantly improved by three new measures introduced by the 1995 Act, principally to relieve the burden of original tenants and their guarantors under old leases but which also benefit new tenancies.[13] In order to avoid the problems created by privity of contract, an original tenant wishing to dispose of the premises should perhaps consider underletting rather than assigning, because then he would at least retain control[14] over the occupier of the premises and be able to exercise all the landlord's remedies against the occupier in the event of default.[15] Where an underlease would not be acceptable, the original tenant should consider inserting in the assignment rights of entry and provisions that would enable the original tenant to require compliance with the terms of the lease and/or making use of the opportunity contained in the Law of Property Act 1925[16] to require that the premises are charged with the payment of all sums that may be payable under an indemnity covenant. The original tenant would then acquire the remedies of a mortgagee.[17]

1   *Baynton v Morgan* (1888) 22 QBD 74, CA; *Thames Manufacturing Co Ltd v Perrotts (Nichol & Peyton) Ltd* (1984) 271 Estates Gazette 284. See, for example, *Weaver v Mogford* [1988] 2 EGLR 48, [1988] 31 EG 49, CA. It follows that the original tenant's guarantor (where there was one) will also be liable: see *Selous Street Properties Ltd v Oronel Fabrics Ltd* (1984) 270 Estates Gazette 643.
2   Ie the landlord for the time being: see Law of Property Act 1925, s 141 (37 *Halsbury's Statutes* (4th edn) REAL PROPERTY); *Re King, Robinson v Gray* [1963] Ch 459, [1963] 1 All ER 781, CA; *Arlesford Trading Co Ltd v Servansingh* [1971] 3 All ER 113, [1971] 1 WLR 1080, CA.
3   The liability remains even if the original tenant has not covenanted on behalf of itself and its successors in title: see Law of Property Act 1925, s 79.
4   The liability remains notwithstanding the death of the original tenant: see para 5.6.6, note 13 above. Furthermore, where an assignee goes bankrupt and his trustee in bankruptcy disclaims the lease, the original tenant will remain liable for rent accruing after the disclaimer: *Warnford Investments Ltd v Duckworth* [1979] Ch 127, [1978] 2 All ER 517. See also *Hindcastle Ltd v Barbara Attenborough Associates Ltd* [1996] 2 WLR 262; *WH Smith Ltd v Wyndham Investments Ltd* [1994] EGCS 94. If the lease is extended, the original tenant's liability will continue: see *Baker v Merckel* [1960] 1 QB 657, [1960] 1 All ER 668, CA. It will not apply where the lease is renewed. As to the court's powers to require guarantors on a lease being renewed under the 1954 Act, see para 14.61 below.

5   The 1995 Act restricts the liability of a former tenant and his guarantor if a lease is varied on or after 1 January 1996 (see para 5.14.3 below). As to the date from which interest is payable under the Supreme Court Act 1981 on sums payable by the original tenant following an assignee's default, see *Allied London Investments Ltd v Hambro Life Assurance Ltd* [1985] 1 EGLR 45, 274 Estates Gazette 148, CA.

6   *Norwich Union Life Insurance Society v Low Profile Fashions Ltd* [1992] 1 EGLR 86, [1992] 21 EG 104. But note the restrictions on landlords' rights to recover rent and service charge from original tenants and their guarantors introduced by the Landlord and Tenant (Covenants) Act 1995, s 17 referred to at para 5.14.1 below.

7   The liability *will* extend to the statutory extension (but *not* to the payment of an interim rent unless this is expressly dealt with), only if the term is defined to include any statutory extension: *City of London Corpn v Fell, Herbert Duncan Ltd v Cluttons* [1993] QB 589, [1993] 2 All ER 449. Apparently if the lease contains a covenant to pay an interim rent, the original tenant *will* be liable.

8   Ie implied by Law of Property Act 1925, s 77 and the Land Registration Act 1925, s 24 (37 *Halsbury's Statutes* (4th edn) REAL PROPERTY). Note also *Moule v Garrett* (1872) LR 7 Ex 101; *Re Healing Research Trustee Co Ltd* [1992] 2 EGLR 231.

9   The indemnity should apply to breaches occurring at any time during the remainder of the term, which will include breaches by the immediate assignee or any subsequent assignee. The original assignee will, in effect, be giving to the original tenant a guarantee (in the form of an indemnity) against breaches by subsequent assignees and as such the original assignee may be tempted to try to limit its liability to breaches occurring while it is the tenant. By privity of estate, an assignee will be liable to the landlord only for breaches of covenant that occur while it holds the lease (*Valliant v Dodemede* (1742) 2 Atk 546) but landlords of old leases will continue to seek to obtain direct covenants from each assignee to observe the provisions of the lease during the remainder of the term. As Asquith J pointed out in *J Lyons & Co Ltd v Knowles* as reported in [1942] 2 All ER 393 at 396, after an assignment there are always two persons liable to be sued for rent, the original tenant who is liable by privity of contract and the assignee who is liable by privity of estate, but by taking the precaution of obtaining direct covenants from assignees (and undertenants) the number of such persons can be increased almost indefinitely.

10   On an assignment there will usually be an indemnity in respect of future breaches given by the assignee to the assignor. The original tenant could be in difficulties where the immediate assignee is insolvent or has ceased to exist because in *RPH v Mirror Group Holdings Ltd* [1993] 1 EGLR 74, [1993] 13 EG 113 the court was not prepared to allow the original tenant to 'leapfrog' the insolvent immediate assignee and to be indemnified by a subsequent solvent assignee.

11   See eg *Selous Street Properties Ltd v Oronel Fabrics Ltd* (1984) 270 Estates Gazette 643; *Thames Manufacturing Co Ltd v Perrotts (Nichol & Peyton) Ltd* (1984) 271 Estates Gazette 284. See also *Weaver v Mogford* [1988] 2 EGLR 48, [1988] 31 EG 49, CA; *Becton Dickinson UK Ltd v Zwebner* [1989] QB 208, [1989] 1 EGLR 71. See also *Mytre Investments Ltd v Reynolds* [1995] 43 EG 131 and *Burford Midland Properties Ltd v Mosley Extensions Ltd* [1995] 30 EG 89.

12   See para 5.8 above.

13   Considered in detail at para 5.14 below.

14   The lack of control which the original tenant can exercise over the current assignee is one of the very real concerns of the concept of continuing liability, because only when the original tenant makes a payment to the landlord will it have any rights to enforce either by virtue of the indemnities or by subrogation (see *Duncan, Fox & Co v North and South Wales Bank* (1880) 6 App Cas 1 HL; *Selous Street Properties Ltd v Oronel Fabrics Ltd* (1984) 270 Estates Gazette 643 where the question of whether or not the original tenant is subrogated to the landlord's right of distress was left open).

15   This view was advanced by Harman J in *Centrovincial Estates plc v Bulk Storage Ltd* (1983) 268 Estates Gazette 59 at 60.

16   Ie Law of Property Act 1925, s 77(7) (37 *Halsbury's Statutes* (4th edn) REAL PROPERTY).

17   Ie sale, possession, foreclosure and the appointment of a receiver.

5.13   *New Tenancies – tenant release.* The basic rule under the 1995 Act is that the tenant will be released from his covenants automatically upon a lawful assignment of the whole of the property demised to him[1] and will have no continuing liability in respect of any breaches of covenant by his successors. There are two main exceptions to this basic rule:

5.13.1   *Excluded assignments.* An assignment in breach of covenant or by operation of law (eg on the death or bankruptcy of the tenant) will not release the outgoing tenant.[2] Here the tenant will remain liable concurrently with the assignee until the next assignment which is not an excluded assignment[3] (whereupon the landlord can require both the first tenant and his assignee to enter into authorised guarantee agreements for the new tenant[4]). An assignor will need to take express indemnities from his assignee where an excluded assignment is made intentionally because the statutory indemnities do not apply to new tenancies.[5]

5.13.2   *Authorised guarantee agreements.* The landlord may require an outgoing tenant to enter into an authorised guarantee agreement[6] by which the tenant guarantees the due performance by his immediate assignee of the obligations on the part of the tenant contained in the lease.[7] The landlord can require the outgoing tenant to enter into an authorised guarantee agreement if:[8]

(a)   the lease absolutely prohibits assignment, but the landlord decides to allow the assignment; or

(b)   the lease allows assignment with the landlord's consent, and it is reasonable for the landlord to require an authorised guarantee agreement;[9] or

(c)   the lease contains a specific provision requiring the giving of an authorised guarantee agreement.[10]

What may – and what must not – be included in the authorised guarantee agreement is prescribed by the 1995 Act.[11] The agreement must not impose on the tenant any requirement to guarantee the performance of any person other than his immediate assignee nor should it impose any liability, restriction or other requirement in relation to any time after the immediate assignee is released by the Act from his obligations under the lease. The 1995 Act specifically permits the guarantee, however, to require the outgoing tenant, in his capacity as guarantor, to take up a new lease should the tenancy be disclaimed on the bankruptcy or liquidation of the assignee.[12] An outgoing tenant should be sure to take an express indemnity from his assignee since the statutory indemnities on assignment of the lease no longer apply to new tenancies.[13]

1   1995 Act, s 5 (23 *Halsbury's Statutes* (4th edn) LANDLORD AND TENANT). The use of the words 'demised to him' in s 5(1) is clearly an error since on a strict interpretation this would limit the release to original tenants only. This was certainly not the intention. If challenged, the preamble to the 1995 Act and reference to *Hansard* under the rule in *Pepper v Hart* [1993] 1 All ER 42 should ensure that the section is interpreted to include all tenants.

2   Ibid, s 11(1).

3   Ibid, s 11(2).

4   Ibid, s 16(6).
5   See ibid, s 14.
6   See ibid, s 16. See also Appendix 1, Form 1.1, Schedule 1.
7   It should be noted that the requirement to provide an authorised guarantee agreement can be in addition to the requirement for a third party contractual guarantor.
8   See ibid, s 16(3).
9   Eg where the assignee's status is questionable.
10   See para 7.5A below.
11   1995 Act, s 16(4) and (5) (23 *Halsbury's Statutes* (4th edn) LANDLORD AND TENANT).
12   See ibid, s 16(5)(c).
13   See note 5 above.

5.14 *New protection for former tenants and their guarantors of all leases.* The 1995 Act has introduced three new measures to protect former tenants and their guarantors. Whilst principally intended to lessen the burden of original tenant liability in old leases, the provisions apply equally to new tenancies.

5.14.1 *Default Notices.*[1] The 1995 Act provides that former tenants[2] shall not be liable to pay any amount in respect of any fixed charge[3] due under the lease unless, within the period of six months[4] beginning with the date on which the charge becomes due, the landlord serves a notice on the former tenant in the prescribed form.[5] Whilst the new provision is clearly to the former tenant's good, there may be an unfortunate side effect for current tenants in default in that landlords may no longer permit late payments or payment by instalments by defaulting tenants. Landlords must serve the default notice within six months of the fixed charge falling due or lose the right to recover from the former tenant.

5.14.2 *Overriding leases.* A former tenant or guarantor who makes a payment pursuant to a default notice will become entitled to an overriding lease[6] interposed between the interest of the landlord and the lease held by the defaulting tenant. The overriding lease will be for a term equal to the remainder of the term of the lease plus (normally) three days,[7] containing essentially the same provisions as those of the current lease,[8] subject to any changes which the parties agree.[9] The overriding lease must also include a statement[10] that it is an overriding lease and indicate whether or not it is a new tenancy for the purposes of the 1995 Act. Landlords should consider their position very carefully before serving a default notice since the grant of an overriding lease may lead to consequences which the landlord might not have contemplated, for example:

(a) the covenant of the person to whom the overriding lease must be granted may not be as strong as the covenant of the current tenant (or others liable to the landlord for payment of the rent and performance of the tenant's covenants). Where the tenancy is an old lease and there is more than one former tenant and guarantor, the landlord should ensure that a default notice is served only on the former tenant or guarantor whom the landlord would be willing to have as tenant under an overriding lease;

(b) there might be collusion between the current and a former tenant to the detriment of the landlord. The current tenant might deliberately withhold payment of the rent, with a view to the landlord making a claim against the former tenant. The former tenant, having then acquired the overriding lease, could accept a surrender of, or forfeit, the lease, and then itself go into liquidation;[11] or

(c) if a lease prohibits subletting there will be no clause requiring any subtenant to obtain the superior landlord's consent to an assignment. Consequently, if the current tenant defaults and, following service of a default notice, the former tenant takes an overriding lease, that overriding lease will not permit subletting unless it has been modified by agreement. Thus the former tenant or guarantor might allow the defaulting tenant to assign without superior landlord's consent. In addition, and of paramount importance to the former tenant or guarantor, is his inability to sublet following forfeiture for breach of covenant by the current tenant.

Similarly, former tenants or guarantors should not rush into overriding leases without proper consideration. Although the overriding lease will give the former tenant control over the current tenant, there may be disadvantages. For example, the terms of the lease may have become more onerous or there may be substantial landlord's obligations which the former tenant may not want to take on. In addition, the former tenant should bear in mind the legal costs and Stamp Duty which will be payable on the grant of the overriding lease.

5.14.3 *Variation of leases.* The 1995 Act restricts the liability of a former tenant or his guarantor if a lease is varied on or after 1 January 1996.[12] A former tenant who remains liable[13] will not be liable to pay any amount to the extent to which that amount is referable to any relevant variation of the tenancy effected after the assignment. A variation is a relevant variation if the landlord has, at the time of the variation (or had immediately before the former tenant assigned the lease), an absolute right to refuse to allow it. For example, a lease when granted might have had a clause limiting the tenant's use of the property to a particular trade or business. If the landlord, being entitled to refuse to agree to the variation, agreed to vary the user clause so as to permit a wider range of uses and this resulted in an increased rent on review, the former tenant would not be liable for the increased rent. A variation extending the term of the lease or the extent of the demised premises will operate as an implied surrender and re-grant.[14] Not only will this release former tenants and guarantors absolutely, it will also create a new tenancy thus giving the current tenant the benefit of automatic release on assignment, etc.

1   See the 1995 Act, s 17 (23 *Halsbury's Statutes* (4th edn) LANDLORD AND TENANT).

2   Whether under original tenant liability or an authorised guarantee agreement. The protection is also afforded to guarantors of former tenants (see para 5.8(d) above), 1995 Act, s 17(1), (3). The landlord's obligation to serve a default notice on guarantors does not apply while the person they are

guaranteeing is the current tenant. For this reason outgoing tenants should consider inserting into authorised guarantee agreements (and contractual guarantors consider inserting into contractual guarantees) an additional clause requiring the landlord to serve a default notice in respect of any fixed sums due under the lease and excluding the landlord's right of recovery where the default notice has not been served within six months of the fixed charge falling due (for a precedent clause see Butterworth's *Encyclopaedia of Forms and Precedents*, Volume 22 (Landlord and Tenant) (5th edn), Form 225.7).

3   'Fixed charges' are: rent, service charge, liquidated damages specified under the lease, and interest on any of these items (1995 Act, s 17(2)(b), 3(b), (6)). The landlord must serve a notice in respect of each payment due, although a single notice may cover more than one payment if they were all due less than six months ago. If the amount due is subject to determination (eg on a rent review) the notice must make this clear and a further notice must be served within three months from when the amount due is finally known (ibid, s 17(4)).

4   Landlords should note that the notice period is calculated in months. If the current tenant has failed to pay the rent due on the March quarter day, it will be too late for the landlord to serve a default notice on the former tenant by the time the September quarter day comes around.

5   For the prescribed form see 22 *Encyclopaedia of Forms and Precedents* (5th edn) Forms 225.9 and 225.10. In relation to the service of the notice the Landlord and Tenant Act 1927, s 23 (23 *Halsbury's Statutes* (4th edn) LANDLORD AND TENANT) will apply (1995 Act, s 27(5)). In view of the importance of the notice, former tenants and guarantors should ensure that they notify the landlord of any changes of address.

6   See 1995 Act, s 19.

7   Or, where the landlord's interest is leasehold, the longest period less than three days that will not wholly displace the landlord's reversionary interest expectant on the current tenancy (see the 1995 Act, s 19(2)(a)).

8   Ibid, s 19(2)(b).

9   Ibid, s 19(2)(b).

10   The statement required by ibid, s 20(2), must be in the following form: 'This lease is granted under section 19 of the 1995 Act and is (*or* is not) a new tenancy for the purposes of section 1 of that Act' (Land Registration (Overriding Leases) Rules 1995/3154, r 2).

11   Landlords' solicitors should consider inserting in leases covenants on the part of the tenant not to accept a surrender of, or forfeit or otherwise determine, any underlease without the consent of the landlord. This provision would then have to be repeated in any overriding lease, but it would not prevent the possibility of the tenant under the overriding lease bringing the original lease to an end, albeit in breach of covenant.

12   1995 Act, s 18. This provision was intended to relieve the liability imposed by *Selous Street Properties Ltd v Oronel Fabrics Ltd* [1984] 1 EGLR 361 and *Centrovincial Estates plc v Bulk Storage Ltd* [1983] 46 P & CR 393, by virtue of which an original tenant remained liable even if the terms of the lease had been varied after disposal in a way not contemplated by the original contract. In fact the more recent case of *Friends Provident Life Office v British Railways Board* [1995] NPC 143, CA altered that understanding of the law and is in line with the provisions of the 1995 Act. The decision is nevertheless important as it renders the freezing date of 1 January 1996 for old variations irrelevant (see 22 *Encyclopaedia of Forms and Precedents (5th edn)* para 56.30).

13   By virtue of original tenant liability under an old lease or under the terms of an authorised guarantee agreement.

14   1995 Act, s 1(5).

5.14A   *A two-tier market?* At the date of this Supplement it is too early to predict whether a two-tier market will be created by the 1995 Act (old leases and new tenancies). New lease clauses have been drafted but they have not yet been tested in the market place or before the courts and there is still uncertainty as to the scope and effect of several key provisions of the 1995 Act. It should not be assumed that prospective tenants will be put off taking assignments of old leases after 1 January 1996, particularly where the term remaining is relatively short.

5.21   **Add:** '1A' after the word 'rent' in the first line.

Add: 1A   Occasionally the reddendum may also impose an obligation on the tenant to pay service charge. In *Royton Industries Ltd v Lawrence* [1994] EGCS 37 the expression 'AND ALSO YIELDING AND PAYING ... the Tenant's proportion of the maintenance costs', contained in the reddendum, was the only obligation relating to service charge in the lease (there was no specific tenant's covenant to pay service charge). Nevertheless, the reddendum was held to impose an express obligation on the tenant to pay service charge, binding on the former tenant by privity of contract after assignment.

Chapter 6

Rent review

6.3   **Delete** from: 'while stressing ...' to 'and two other topics' and **replace** with 'has confirmed that it has no current intention to legislate in relation to existing leases but a Code¹ has been introduced dealing with upwards-only rent review clauses and two other topics'.

1   **Delete** entirely and **replace** with: 1 See para 1.6A above.

6.5.3   **Insert** '19A' after the words 'when the term is being continued by the 1954 Act'.

Add: 19A   *Willison v Cheverell Estates Ltd* [1995] EGCS 111, CA.

6.6   **Add:** The tenant should avoid a clause by which the review process can only be instigated by the landlord because this could mean that when rental values have fallen, the landlord deliberately fails to instigate a review in the hope that the current rent will continue to be payable.⁹

Add   9   *Harben Style Ltd v Rhodes Trust* [1995] 1 EGLR 118, [1995] 17 EG 125; *Royal Bank of Scotland plc v Jennings* [1995] 2 EGLR 87, [1995] 35 EG 140. See also *GRE Compass Ltd v Drapers Co* [1994] EGCS 97 (dealing with 'one-off' drafting) where a decision not to implement a review (when no increase could have been achieved) did not amount to a 'review' for the purposes of the headlease.

6.10

4   **Delete** entirely and **replace** with:
4   (Time *not* of essence) *Phipps-Faire Ltd v Malbern Construction Ltd* [1987] 1 EGLR 129, 282 Estates Gazette 460; *Power Securities (Manchester) Ltd v Prudential Assurance Co Ltd* [1987] 1 EGLR 121, 281 Estates Gazette 1327; *Panavia Air Cargo Ltd v Southend-on-Sea Borough Council* [1988] 1 EGLR 124, [1988] 22 EG 82, CA; *Henniker-Major v Daniel Smith (a firm)* (1990) 62 P&CR 24, [1991] 1 EGLR 128; *Pembroke St Georges Ltd v Cromwell Developments Ltd* [1991] 2 EGLR 129, [1991] 40 EG 115; *North Hertfordshire District Council v Hitchin Industrial Estate Ltd* [1992] 2 EGLR 121, [1992] 37 EG 133; *Bickenhall Engineering Co Ltd v Grandmet Restaurants Ltd* [1995] 1 EGLR 110, [1995] 10 EG 123. But note (Time of essence) *Mammoth Greeting Cards Ltd v Agra Ltd* [1990] 2 EGLR 124, [1990] 29 EG 45; *Chelsea Building Society v R & A Millett (Shops) Ltd* [1994] 1 EGLR 148, [1994] 09 EG 182 (virtually the same clause as in *North Hertfordshire*, see above, but a different outcome!); *Central Estates Ltd v Secretary of State for the Environment* [1995] EGCS 110, CA.

6.12.6

15   **Add**: Similar principles apply when it is the landlord who has failed within the appropriate period to appoint an arbitrator: *Fordgate (Bingley) Ltd v National Westminster Bank plc* [1995] EGCS 97.

6.19   Add: In *Secretary of State for the Environment v Associated Newspapers Holdings Ltd* [1995] EGCS 166, the landlord still succeeded in spite of 'linguistic overkill' and otiose wording.

6.21

1   **Add:** *Guildford Borough Council v Cobb* [1994] 1 EGLR 156, [1994] 16 EG 147.

2   **Add:** Problems can also arise as to what planning permissions are to be assumed, for example in the case of a lease granted pursuant to a building agreement: *Worcester City Council v AS Clarke (Worcester) Ltd* [1994] EGCS 31.

6.22

1   **Add:** See also *Millshaw Property Co Ltd v Preston Borough Council* [1995] EGCS 186 where the expression 'for a term of years not exceeding the residue of the term' was used.

6.23.3

19   **Add**: Fairly standard provisions can have a potentially onerous effect, for example in the case of an old building or where the duration of the term of the lease is longer than usual: see *Ladbroke Hotels Ltd v Sandhu* [1995] 2 EGLR 92, [1995] 39 EG 152 which concerned the tenant's repairing covenant.

6.23.5

21   **Add:** *Commercial Union Life Assurance Co Ltd v Woolworths plc* [1994] EGCS 191.

6.25

3   **Add:** See also *Ocean Accident & Guarantee Corpn v Next plc* and *Commercial Union Assurance Co plc v Next plc* [1995] EGCS 187 where trade fixtures affixed to the premises by the tenant, even though pursuant to an obligation contained in the lease, would not be expected to enhance the rent.

6.26.2 Delete the paragraph entirely and **replace** with:

6.26.2   *Drafting.* As is the case with many artificial assumptions,[7] it has proved difficult to produce wording that guarantees what the landlord is seeking, and uncertainty has been created as a result, although the Court of Appeal, in the Broadgate case,[8] has given guidance on the wording that would be effective.

8   **Delete** from 'The landlord failed' to 'the tenant will be fitting out or offered as an inducement' and **replace** with '*Broadgate Square plc v Lehman Bros Ltd* [1995] 1 EGLR 97, in which four cases were consolidated into the one appeal – the wording failed to achieve the headline rent on review in the other three cases'.

6.32

1   **Add** the words: 'were still' before the word 'there' in ninth line.

6.33.2

12   **Add**: The approach seen in *Daejan Investments Ltd* (see above) was followed in *Parkside Clubs (Nottingham) Ltd v Armgrade Ltd* [1995] 2 EGLR 96, [1995] EG 104, CA.

6.35

1   **Delete** '2.27 above' and **replace** with '2.26 above'.
2   **Delete** '2.25 above' and **replace** with '2.24 above'.
5   **Delete** '2.26 above' and **replace** with '2.25 above'.
6   **Add** the words 'In the case of old leases' before the words 'Such an obligation'.
     Add: In the case of new tenancies however (where the touch and concern rule is no
     longer relevant) such an obligation by the landlord will pass on an assignment of the
     whole or any part and bind successors in title: Landlord and Tenant (Covenants) Act
     1995, s 3(3). For the distinction between old leases, in respect of which the original
     contracting parties will continue to remain liable throughout the term of the lease,
     and new tenancies which are subject to the Landlord and Tenant (Covenants) Act
     1995, see para 5.11 above.

6.42

2   In the ninth line **delete** '⁶' and **replace** it with a single closed quotation mark; and
     replace the word 'words' with 'works'.
     In the twelfth line **replace** the word 'it' with 'if'. In the last line **delete** '[in the licence
     . . .] . . . redrafted' and **replace** with 'ensuring the provisions such as these (which are
     fairly standard form) are redrafted.'
14   **Add** a new reference for *Historic Houses Hotels Ltd v Cadogan Estates* [1995] 1 EGLR
     117, [1995] 11 EG 140, CA.

6.50   In the twelfth line after the words 'proposing to dispose of the lease'
           add the words 'or where his lease contains an upwards and downwards
           review clause and the market has fallen since the last review date'.

3   **Add:** *Fordgate Bingley Ltd v Argyll Stores Ltd* [1994] 2 EGLR 84, [1994] 39 EG 135.

6.51

3   **Add:** A party's expert in arbitration proceedings can be compelled to produce his
     proofs of evidence in other rent review arbitrations: *London & Leeds Estates Ltd v
     Paribas Ltd (No 2)* [1995] 1 EGLR 102, [1995] 02 EG 134. A similar situation could
     not arise in the case of determination by an expert. As to the admissibility of evidence,
     see *Land Securities plc v Westminster City Council* [1993] 4 All ER 124, [1992] 2 EGLR
     15 which held that in a rent review arbitrators' awards in other reviews are inadmissible.
4   **Add:** For an example of an action for negligence (that failed) by a disgruntled tenant
     against an expert, see *Zubaida v Hargreaves* [1995] 1 EGLR 127, [1995] 09 EG 320.

6.52.2

11   **Add:** See also *Prudential Assurance Co Ltd v Trafalgar House Group Estates Ltd* [1991]
     1 EGLR 127, [1991] 01 EG 103, CA; *Euripides v Gascoigne Holdings Ltd* [1995] EGCS
     119; and *Secretary of State for the Environment v Euston Centre Investments Ltd* [1995]
     Ch 200, [1994] 2 EGLR 20, CA which is an important case as it sets out the governing
     principles underlying the exercise of the court's inherent power.

6.54   **Amend** the second sentence to read 'These sections deal with the power
           of the High Court to remit matters for the reconsideration of the
           arbitrator, ¹ᴬ the removal of an arbitrator...'.

1A   **Add:** Note *Arnold v National Westminster Bank plc* [1993] 1 EGLR 23, [1993] 01 EG
     94; on appeal [1994] EGCS 44 CA; *Broadgate Square plc v Lehman Bros Ltd (No 2)*
     [1995] 2 EGLR 5.
5   **Add:** *Mount Charlotte Investments plc v Prudential Assurance* [1995] 1 EGLR 15, [1995]
     10 EG 129; *Atkinson v WSFS Ltd* [1995] EGCS 152, [1996] 14 EG 94; *Turner v
     Stevenage Borough Council* [1995] EGCS 181; *Techno Ltd v Allied Dunbar Assurance plc*
     [1993] 22 EG 109; *Control Securities plc v Spencer* [1989] 07 EG 82; and *Gladesmore
     Investments Ltd v Caradon Heating Ltd* [1994] 1 EGLR 28, [1994] 15 EG 159, Ch D.

Chapter 7

The tenant's covenants

7.1.1 In the eleventh line **delete** the words 'Even though the original tenant will usually remain liable following assignment,[7] the landlord' and **replace** them with the words: 'Even though a landlord may be able to enforce the tenant's covenants against an original tenant, either by privity of contract[7] or pursuant to the terms of an authorised guarantee agreement,[7A] he ...'

7.1.2 In the first line **replace** the words 'that require' with the word: 'why'.

In the twelfth line **replace** the word 'will' with the word: 'may'.

In the thirteenth line **replace** '[10]' with: '[9A]'.

Add: **7.1.5** *New underlettings granted out of old leases.*[12] Care must be taken where a landlord with an old lease[12] wishes to grant an underlease. The underlease will be a new tenancy[13] even though the lease out of which it is granted is an old lease. Whilst the landlord's lease may contain a provision requiring any underlessee to enter into a direct covenant with the superior landlord for the whole of the term of the underlease, this is now prohibited by statute.[14] A superior landlord may only require an undertenant[15] to covenant for the period during which the undertenant is bound by the tenant's covenants contained in the underlease and for any period during which it is liable under an authorised guarantee agreement.[7A]

7   **Delete** entirely and **replace** with: 7   See para 5.12 above.
Add: 7A   See para 5.13.2 above.

Add: 9A   See paras 5.11 to 5.15 above.
12   For the distinction between old leases, in respect of which the original contracting parties will continue to remain liable throughout the term of the lease, and new tenancies which will be subject to the Landlord and Tenant (Covenants) Act 1995 (23 *Halsbury's Statutes* (4th edn) LANDLORD AND TENANT), see para 5.11 above.
13   Unless it falls within one of the exceptions referred to at para 5.11(a) – (d) above.
14   Landlord and Tenant (Covenants) Act 1995, s 25(1) (23 *Halsbury's Statutes* (4th edn) LANDLORD AND TENANT).
15   The superior landlord may also require successive undertenants to enter into a similar direct covenant.

7.2.1 **Add:** By virtue of a new provision, s 19(1D),[1A] however, building leases which are new tenancies for the purpose of the Landlord and Tenant

(Covenants) Act 1995[1B] will no longer enjoy the benefit of s 19(1)(b) – consent to assignment will be required throughout the term of the lease.

Add: 1A Inserted by Landlord and Tenant (Covenants) Act 1995, s 22 (23 *Halsbury's Statutes* (4th edn) LANDLORD AND TENANT).

1B See para 5.11 above.

7.2.2 In the sixth line **replace** the words 'which is most frequently called' with the words: 'which has most frequently been called'.

Insert additional antepenultimate and penultimate sentences: Like s 19(1)(b), s 19(1)(a) has been amended by the Landlord and Tenant (Covenants) Act 1995.[2A] In respect of new tenancies [2B] landlords may agree in advance the conditions upon which consent to assignment will be given.

In the final sentence, **replace** 'It' with 'The provision, as amended,'.

Add: 2A See Landlord and Tenant Act 1927, s 19(1A) (as inserted by the Landlord and Tenant (Covenants) Act 1995, s 22).

2B See note 1A above. Residential leases, agricultural holdings and farm business tenancies under the Agricultural Tenancies Act 1995 are excluded. See the Landlord and Tenant Act 1927, s 19(1E)(a) (as inserted by the Landlord and Tenant (Covenants) Act 1995, s 22) and the Landlord and Tenant Act 1927, s 19(4) (as amended).

7.5 In the fifteenth line, after the end of the sixth sentence, **insert** a new sentence: Although in respect of new tenancies, where there is a qualified prohibition against assignment, the landlord and tenant may now agree in advance the terms upon which consent to assignment will be given,[7A] as explained in para 7.5A below.

In the thirtieth line, **replace** the words 'Any attempt' with the words 'Except in the circumstances referred to at para 7.5A below, any attempt'.

Add: 7A See also para 7.2.2 above.

12 **Add**: Note too *Olympia & York Ltd v Oil Property Investment Ltd* [1994] 29 EG 121. See also *Beale v Worth; King v Same; Reynolds v Same* [1993] EGCS 135.

Add: 7.5A *New tenancies and conditions for assignment.* New provisions have been introduced into s 19(1) of the 1927 Act[1] which, in relation to new tenancies[2] only, enable a landlord and tenant to agree[3] the circumstances in which the landlord may withhold consent to an assignment, or the conditions subject to which consent may be granted.[4] If these circumstances or conditions are framed by reference to any matter falling to be determined by the landlord, the lease must provide either that the landlord must be reasonable or that the tenant has the unrestricted right to have any such determination reviewed by an independent third party whose determination will be conclusive.[5] If consent is refused in these specified circumstances, or if the specified conditions are imposed to a consent, the consent will not have been unreasonably withheld. Assignment provisions in new tenancies will almost certainly include an explicit requirement that the outgoing tenant enter into an authorised guarantee agreement,[6] whereby he will remain liable for any breach of covenant by his immediate assignee. What additional conditions are imposed will depend on the circumstances of the letting but landlords should be wary of drawing up a draconian set of preconditions which may adversely affect the rent on review.[7]

1   Landlord and Tenant Act 1927, s 19(1A)–(1E) (as inserted by the Landlord and Tenant (Covenants) Act 1995, s 22).
.2   See para 5.11 above.
3   Agreement may be in the lease itself or be added by a later document provided that it pre-dates the tenant's application for consent for the assignment, Landlord and Tenant Act 1927, s 19(1B).
4   Landlord and Tenant Act 1927, s 19(1A).
5   Landlord and Tenant Act 1927, s 19(1C). See also Appendix 1, Form 1.1, clause 9.4.
6   See para 5.13.2 above.
7   It is suggested that conditions should ideally be few in number and easy to operate. A condition requiring that any assignee be of similar financial standing to the original tenant may seem innocuous enough but, depending on the identity of the original tenant, may be a difficult criterion to meet. Conditions which may effectively prevent assignment may lead to a discounted rent at review.
    In January 1996 a working party of the Association of British Insurers (comprising a number of major funds with property portfolios) produced a set of working draft clauses for inclusion in new leases. The working party's aim was to exercise sufficient control over assignments to prevent a significant increase in the risks to cashflow, whilst avoiding any adverse impact on rents at review (see Report of the ABI Working Party on the Landlord and Tenant (Covenants) Act 1995, January 1996). The clauses provide a sound basis for landlords wishing to protect themselves and have been incorporated, with minor amendment, in Appendix 1 Form 1.1 below (at clauses 9.2.3 and 9.3). Some landlords may wish to impose more rigorous controls and try and avoid any depressing effect upon the rent on review by inserting an appropriate disregard in the rent review clause (though tenants would be likely to challenge any such provision and it remains to be seen whether the courts, in due course, would view such a disregard as effective).

7.6

11   **Add:** *Dong Bang Minerva (UK) Ltd v Devina Ltd* [1995] 5 EG 162, Hazel Williamson QC (sitting as a Deputy Judge of the Chancery Division) held that a landlord was in breach of its statutory duty and that in seeking consent to the proposed transaction, the tenant did not have to undertake to be responsible for the landlord's costs. She felt that if a landlord has been furnished with sufficient particulars of the proposed transaction, such as agreed heads of terms, the landlord would know the substance of the true nature of the transaction so as to be able to make a sensible decision on its merits although that consent may well be subject to further approval of the form of sublease. Even if there were cases in which the landlord was entitled to require an undertaking for his costs, this could only apply where the undertaking so requested was for a reasonable sum or reasonable costs. Consent had been applied for in letters dated 6 and 7 July and the judge felt that on the facts, the landlord ought to have been able to give a conditional consent by, at the latest, 8 August.

15   **Add**: Landlord and Tenant Act 1988, s 1(3) takes effect subject to the provisions of Landlord and Tenant (Covenants) Act 1995 (ie the Landlord and Tenant Act 1927, s 19(1A) as inserted). Hence the question of what is a reasonable time for responding to a request for consent may depend upon the complexity of the conditions subject to which consent may be granted and the amount of information which has been supplied to the landlord.

7.7.2 **Replace** the second and third sentences with: Old leases [14A] frequently contain an additional requirement [15] to the effect that any assignee will covenant direct with the landlord to pay the rent and perform and observe the covenants during the residue of the term.[16] There are essentially two reasons why landlords imposed such a requirement: to ensure that there was no question of the assignee arguing that he was not bound by a particular covenant because it did not touch and concern the land,[17] and to give the assignee an incentive not to assign to a person of poor financial standing, by rendering the assignee liable following further assignment.[18]

Add after the end of the third sentence: Whilst this practice remains lawful in respect of old leases, the same is not true of new tenancies.[14A] The distinction between covenants which touch and concern the land and those which do not has been abolished in respect of new tenancies.[18A] The Landlord and Tenant (Covenants) Act 1995 prevents a landlord from requiring direct covenants from assignees [18B] and thus attempting to recreate privity of contract. The basic rule of the 1995 Act is that tenants under new tenancies are automatically released from the tenant's covenants on lawful assignment and no longer have to underwrite their successors.[18C] One of the exceptions to this rule is the ability of the landlord to require an outgoing tenant to enter into an authorised guarantee agreement[18D] by which the outgoing tenant is required to guarantee its immediate assignee. A landlord may also specify in any new tenancy the terms upon which consent to any assignment will be granted.[18E]

7.7.3.5 Add: By virtue of the Landlord and Tenant (Covenants) Act 1995 an undertenant may only be required to covenant with the landlord for the period during which the undertenant is bound by the tenant's covenants contained in the underlease, and for any period during which he is liable under an authorised guarantee agreement, as explained at para 7.1.5 above.

7.7.1 – 7.7.7

8   **Amend** 'Appendix 1, Form 1.1, clause 9.1' to 'Appendix 1, Form 1.1, clause 9.2'.

12   **Amend** 'Appendix 1, Form 1.1, clause 9.2' to 'Appendix 1, Form 1.1, clause 9.2.2'.

14   **Amend** 'Appendix 1, Form 1.1, clause 9.4' to 'Appendix 1, Form 1.1, clause 9.2.3'.

Add: 14A   For the distinction between old leases and new tenancies for the purpose of the Landlord and Tenant (Covenants) Act 1995, see para 5.11 above.

16   **Delete**: 'See 22 *Encyclopaedia of Forms and Precedents* (5th edn) Form 22, clause 5.9.4; Appendix 1, Form 1.1, clause 9.4'.

18   **Delete** last sentence and **replace** with: For an example of an intermediate assignee being held liable, see *Estates Gazette Ltd v Benjamin Restaurants Ltd* [1994] 1 WLR 1528, [1994] 26 EG 140.

Add: 18A   Landlord and Tenant (Covenants) Act 1995, s 2 (23 *Halsbury's Statutes* (4th edn) LANDLORD AND TENANT). The benefit and burden of all tenant covenants contained in a new tenancy will be annexed and incident to the premises demised by the tenancy and will pass on an assignment of the whole or any part of them, Landlord and Tenants (Covenants) Act 1995, s3(1).

18B   Landlord and Tenant (Covenants) Act 1995, s 25(1) (23 *Halsbury's Statutes* (4th edn) LANDLORD AND TENANT).

18C   Ibid, s 5. See para 5.13 above.

> **18D**   Ibid, s 16. See para. 5.13.2 above.
>
> **18E**   Ibid, s 22. See para 7.5A above.

19   **Delete** 'Appendix 1, Form 1.1, clause 9.5'.

23   **Amend** 'Appendix 1, Form 1.1, clause 9.3' to 'Appendix 1, Form 1.1, clause 9.2.4'.

32   In the sixth line **delete** 'of' and **replace** with : 'as'. In the tenth line **insert** 'having' after the word 'determined'.

33   **Amend** 'Appendix 1, Form 1.1, clause 9.6.1' to 'Appendix 1, Form 1.1, clause 9.5.1.2' and **amend** the subsequent reference, 'Form 1.1, clause 9.6.3' to: 'Form 1.1, clause 9.5.1.4'.

42   **Amend** 'Appendix 1, Form 1.1, clause 9.6.3' to: 'Appendix 1, Form 1.1, clause 9.5.1.4'. and **amend** the subsequent reference, 'Form 1.1, clause 9.6.3', to 'Form 1.1, clause 9.5.1.4'.

49   **Amend** 'Appendix 1, Form 1.1, clause 9.8.1' to 'Appendix 1, Form 1.1, clause 9.5.2.1'. **Add**: See also *Hemingway Securities Ltd v Dunraven Ltd* [1995] 9 EG 322 where a tenant executed a sublease of premises in breach of a precondition contained in the lease requiring that subtenants should enter into a direct covenant with the landlord and that the form of the sublease should be approved by the landlord. The landlord successfully obtained mandatory injunctions against the tenant for breach of contract and against the subtenant for inducing a breach of contract. It was also held that there was no reason why a covenant against alienation could not be a restrictive covenant, binding on the subtenant.

53   **Amend** 'Appendix 1, Form 1.1, clause 9.3' to 'Appendix 1, Form 1.1, clause 9.2.1'.

54   **Amend** 'Form 1.1, clause 5.9.11' to 'Form 1.1, clause 9.2.1'.

55   **Amend** 'Appendix 1, Form 1.1, clause 9.2' to 'Appendix 1, Form 1.1, clause 9.2.2'.

57   **Amend** 'Appendix 1, Form 1.1, clause 9.3' to 'Appendix 1, Form 1.1, clause 9.2.5'.

59   **Amend** 'Appendix 1, Form 1.1, clause 9.9' to 'Appendix 1, Form 1.1, clause 9.7'.

7.15.2 At the end of the first sentence replace the words 'parade or centre.' with 'parade or centre.[6]'

At the beginning of the second sentence **insert** the word 'Generally' and later in the second sentence **amend** '[6]' to become '[6A]'.

At the end of the paragraph **add**: A covenant to keep open during 'normal business hours' will not require the tenant to open the shop on Sundays.[14] However, tenants should bear in mind that leases entered into on or after 26 August 1994 can, subject to negotiation, require a tenant to trade on Sundays.[15]

6   **Delete** the last sentence.

Add: 6A   Damages rather than an injunction or specific performance has usually been the appropriate remedy for breach of a 'keep open' covenant: *Bradden Towers Ltd v International Stores Ltd* [1987] 1 EGLR 209; *FW Woolworth plc v Charlwood Alliance Properties Ltd* [1987] 1 EGLR 53, 282 Estates Gazette 585; Vivien King and Martin Wright: Open All Hours [1995] 13 EG 126. In the case of *Co-Operative Insurance Society Ltd v Argyll Stores (Holdings) Ltd* [1996] 09 Estates Gazette 128, however, the court granted a mandatory injunction requiring a tenant to keep its unit open, enforcing the positive user clause contained in the lease. It is thought that the *Argyll* case is unlikely to lead to an injunction being available in every case as the circumstances were exceptional: the premises formed the anchor unit of a shopping centre; the tenant was a major retailer; the other tenants of the centre would suffer as a result of the tenant's breach (without being entitled to legal recourse) so that damages would be hard to quantify; and, whilst the landlord had acted promptly to try to avert the tenant's breach (suggesting a rent concession), the tenant had acted with what was described by Lord Justice Leggatt as 'unmitigated commercial cynicism'. Interestingly though in *Retail Parks Investments Ltd v Royal Bank of Scotland plc* (1995) SLT 1156 (OH) an interim order was granted in favour of the landlord of a shopping centre ordering a banking tenant to keep premises open for business as bank offices during normal business hours pending the resolution of a dispute as to the extent of the bank's obligations under the lease.

Add: 14   Sunday Trading Act 1994, s 3.

15   Conceivably this may cause difficulties in respect of shopping centres where leases were granted both before and after the Sunday Trading Act 1994. If only some tenants can be required by the landlord to trade on Sundays, there is likely to be uncertainty as to whether the landlord can recover the costs of opening the centre from all of the tenants or only those required to trade. Landlords should ensure that this point is specifically addressed when drafting service charge provisions in new leases.

7.16.3

10   **Add**: See also *Barclays Bank plc v Daejan Investments (Grove Hall) Ltd* [1995] 18 EG 117 discussed at [1995] 15 EG 108.

17   **Add**: In *Chesterfield MH Investments v British Gas plc* [1995] (Unreported, ChD) a pre-trial injunction was granted to the landlord to prevent the tenant from operating its business in breach of the user covenant. The covenant was fully qualified and the judge held that an unreasonable withholding of consent by the landlord to a change of use would free the covenantor from compliance. The onus was on the covenantor, however, to show that the refusal was outside the band of possible decisions that a reasonable landlord would make.

Add: 7.26A   *The Disability Discrimination Act 1995.*   This new statute imposes a duty on employers[1] (and this could include a tenant) to take reasonable steps to prevent any physical features of the premises occupied by the employer placing a disabled person at a substantial disadvantage in comparison with able-bodied persons.[2]

Where an employer occupies premises under a lease which prohibits the tenant from making alterations, thereby precluding the employer from complying with its obligations to take 'reasonable steps', a consent procedure in respect of the necessary alterations is implied into the lease by the new Act.[3] Where consent is sought and refused, either the complainant or the occupier may ask the industrial tribunal to direct that the landlord be joined as a party to any proceedings brought against the employer alleging discrimination on grounds of disability. This may result in the landlord being obliged to consent to the alterations and being ordered to pay compensation to the complainant.

There is a provision in the new Act for regulations to be made relating to the circumstances in which consent may be withheld but those regulations have not yet been put in place. It will be important for landlords to bear in mind developments in the law in this area and to be mindful of the possible consequences of refusing consent where the purpose for which that consent has been sought is to accommodate the needs of the disabled worker.

1   Parallel provisions apply to 'trade organisations', defined in the Disability Discrimination Act 1995, s 13(4) as an organisation of workers or employers or other organisation whose members carry on a particular profession or trade for the purposes of which the organisation exists.

2   Disability Discrimination Act 1995, s 6 (employers); s 15 (trade organisations).

3   Save to the extent that the lease expressly so provides, Disability Discrimination Act 1995, s 16.

7.27   In the eighteenth line **delete** the sentence beginning 'Materials in waste ...' and **replace** it with 'Materials in waste can form leachate, while methane gas given off during organic decomposition can migrate and explode.'

5   **Delete** the last sentence.

7.28   Delete '³' from the fifth line of the paragraph.

Delete '⁴' from the tenth line of the paragraph.

In the eleventh line of the paragraph, **renumber** '⁵' as '³'.

In the last line of the paragraph **replace** the words 'consequences or ignoring it' with 'consequences of ignoring it'.

3   **Delete** entirely.
4   **Delete** entirely.
5   **Renumber** as '³' and **delete** the last sentence.

7.29.1 **Replace** the paragraph with:

> **7.29.1**   *Environmental Protection Act 1990, Part IIA.* The Environment Act 1995[1] introduced a new Part IIA into the Environmental Protection Act 1990. It confers extensive powers (and some duties) on both local authorities and the Environment Agency[2] in relation to contaminated land. The provisions are expected to come into force later in 1996 and depend on regulations and guidance which have yet to appear in their final form. Local authorities will have responsibility for most of the contaminated land which falls within the statutory definition,[3] while the Environment Agency will deal with so-called 'special sites'[4] (where there is heavy contamination). The provisions are similar to the statutory nuisance regime under Part III of the 1990 Act. Clean-up is effected by means of the actual or threatened service of remediation notices.[5] These are served, in the first instance, on the person who caused or knowingly permitted the contamination; but if that person, after reasonable inquiry, cannot be found service can be effected on the owner or occupier. There are various exceptions and qualifications which are designed to give effect to the government's twin aim to ensure that:
>
> (a)   land is cleaned up only where it represents a real risk to human health and environment (and then only to make it suitable for its current use); and
> (b)   the polluter pays rather than the innocent landowner.
>
> Whether this is how the broad provisions are actually implemented remains to be seen.

7.29.2 After the words 'National Rivers Authority', in the second line of the paragraph, **add** '(from 1 April 1996, the Environment Agency)'.

After the words '... timely remedial action.' , in the eigth line **add** 'Clean up can now be effected also by means of works notices which were introduced by the Environment Act 1995.'

7.29.3 **Replace** the paragraph with:

7.29.3 *Statutory nuisances.* The statutory nuisance provisions in Part III of the Environmental Protection Act 1990 were previously believed to have at least some potential application to contaminated land (even though in practice they tended to be used only for more mundane problems such as noise, dust and smell). The definition of the statutory nuisance will shortly exclude land which is in a contaminated state (a definition based on but broader than the definition of contaminated land in Part IIA of the 1990 Act as described above).

7.29.1 – 7.29.3

1–7	**Delete** entirely and replace with:

    1   See Environment Act 1995, s 57.

    2   The Environment Act 1995, s 1 provides for the creation of the Environment Agency whilst s 2 deals with the transfer of functions, property, rights and liabilities to the Agency.

    3   Environmental Protection Act 1990, s 78A(2) (as inserted by the Environment Act 1995, s 57).

    4   Environmental Protection Act 1990, s 78A(3) (as inserted by the Environment Act 1995, s 57).

    5   Environmental Protection Act 1990, s 78E (as inserted by the Environment Act 1995, s 57).

12–19 **Delete** entirely.

7.29.4

20   Amend '1993' to '1994'.

7.30.1 In the twenty-sixth line of the paragraph **amend** the words 'int he' to 'in the'.

7.30.4

16   **Delete** from 'Lord Goff pointed out...' to '... March 1994'.

7.32.1 In the fourth line of the paragraph, after the words 'regulatory authorities', **add** '(including, from 1 April 1996, the Environment Agency)'.

In the third and sixth lines of the paragraph **delete** '3'.

7.32.3 In the eleventh line of the paragraph **delete** '4'.

3   **Delete** entirely.
4   **Delete** entirely.

7.33

4   **Delete** last sentence.

7.34 In the final sentence of the paragraph, **delete** '3'.

3   **Delete** entirely.

7.35 In the fourth line of the paragraph, **delete** '2'.

2   **Delete** entirely.

Add: **7.37A** *CDM Regulations.* Where works are to be carried out at the premises, the CDM Regulations[1] which place formal health and safety obligations upon all parties involved in the procurement process (whether that be new build, refurbishment, maintenance and/or repair) will in all probability apply.[2]

A 'client' under the CDM Regulations is 'anyone for whom a project is carried out' and could, by definition, include owners, occupiers, joint venture partners and those funding the works; and with sanctions for breach being harsh[3], the CDM Regulations do require careful consideration where works are to be undertaken. The 'client's' duties relate to its appointees pursuant to the Regulations (ie the planning supervisor,[4] the principal contractor and designers). The client will need to be reasonably satisfied as to the competence and experience of its appointees and needs to take reasonable steps to ascertain what resources allocated by those appointees will be adequate to fulfill their functions under the Regualtions. The provision of information to the planning supervisor is another function of the client. A health and safety file[5] (rather like an operation and maintenance manual) is to be passed on to any subsequent purchasers of the building and as such it will be important for the freeholder to keep the document.

1   The Construction (Design and Management) Regulations 1994. See the Approved Code of Practice (ACOP) published by the Health and Safety Commission for advice on how to comply with the law. ACOP has a special legal status – if it can be proved that the relevant provisions of ACOP have not been followed, this will be deemed to be a breach of the CDM Regulations unless it can be demonstrated that compliance was achieved in some other way.

2   There are works which will be excluded. See reg 3 of the CDM Regulations and ACOP.

3   Sanctions for breach are governed by the Health and Safety at Work etc Act 1974 enforceable by criminal law with a penalty of an unlimited fine or up to two years' imprisonment. There are instances which may give rise to breach of statutory duty (ie civil liability) for example the client is to ensure as far as reasonably practicable that the construction phase does not start unless a health and safety plan has been prepared.

4   This new role has been created by the CDM Regulations, the planning supervisor being responsible for co-ordinating health and safety aspects of design and planning.

5   Which will contain information about materials, techniques used in construction and information about health and safety matters affecting the building, for example about the structure and services (including plant).

Chapter 8

Repairing covenants

8.1

10   **Add**: *Secretary of State for the Environment v Euston Centre Investments Ltd (No 2)* [1994] EGCS 167.

8.2

5   Note new **reference** for *Credit Suisse v Beegas Nominees Ltd*: [1994] 4 All ER 803.

     Add: A covenant in a lease to keep the property in 'complete, good and substantial repair and condition' obliges the landlord to keep the property in repair at all times so that there is a breach immediately the defect occurs: *British Telecom plc v Sun Life Assurance Society plc* [1995] EGCS 139. See para 8.27 below.

8.4

3   **Add**: The curse of the black spot: condensation and the law [1995] 13 EG 128, 15 EG 103.

6   **Add**: ;*Secretary of State for the Environment v Euston Centre Investments Ltd (No 2)* [1994] EGCS 167.

8.16.1   In the fourth line after 'of the development[4]' **add** 'who may acquire an interest in the development of the works'.

     In the fifth line after the words 'professional team ('the warrantor')' **add** ', being collateral to the building contract or professional appointment,'.

8.17.1

3   **Delete** entirely and **replace** with: 'See paras 5.11–5.14 above in respect of the changes which have been made to privity of contract in relation to landlord and tenant law.

8.17.3   In the second line **delete** 'Foundation 15' and **replace** with 'their three current competitors, Zurich Municipal with a scheme launched in 1993, SHIELD set up in 1995 and HAPM[4A] offering'.

Add   **4A**   HAPM is a mutual insurance club for housing association members and offers a 35 year latent defects insurance.

5   **Delete** entirely and **replace** with: 'Although more readily available in the UK, latent defects insurance policies still offer limited scope of cover and command a high premium. They are usually taken out by the developer/building owner at the design stage and may involve a technical audit on behalf of the insurer. Developers should consult their insurance brokers to ascertain the viability of such schemes. See R Grover 'Insurance: Latent Defects and Consequential Loss' [1990] 11 EG 102.

8.19

3   **Add**: See also the effect of *Jervis v Harris* [1995] ECGS 177 (CA) on the 1938 Act, considered at para 8.22A below.

Add: **8.22A**   *The effect of Jervis v Harris.*[1] The protection afforded to tenants by the 1938 Act has been substantially reduced by the recent case of *Jervis v Harris* in which it was established that a landlord need not obtain leave of the court to take action for reimbursement of expenses incurred in carrying out repairs which were the obligation of the tenant under the lease, where the landlord had properly entered the property under a power contained in the lease. The Court of Appeal held that the tenant's liability was for reimbursement of a debt due, not damages in compensation of the breach of the tenant's repairing covenant.[2] In the present market this decision will be welcomed by landlords wishing to preserve their investment but reluctant to take forfeiture proceedings. In future, landlords will wish to ensure that enter, repair and charge clauses are widely drafted[3] and that there are no provisions in the lease limiting the landlord's right of recovery to damages.[4] Tenants, on the other hand, will try to resist the imposition of enter, repair and charge clauses in new leases or, where that is not possible, insist upon amendment to preserve the spirit of the 1938 Act. Similarly, tenants will wish to limit the amount of expenditure which a landlord can recover under such clauses to the equivalent of the diminution in value of the reversion caused by the want of repair as it is uncertain what effect the decision in *Jervis v Harris* may have on s 18 of the Landlord and Tenant Act 1927 (discussed at para 8.23 below). Whilst this self-help remedy will give landlords a new option where tenants are in breach of their repairing obligations, careful consideration will still be required before any expenditure is incurred. The financial standing of a tenant may be precarious, in which case taking action for recovery of expenditure incurred by the landlord may only lead to the tenant's insolvency. The landlord should also bear in mind that if he wishes to be able to recover his expenditure from any former tenant[5], he will need to serve a default notice[6] or lose his rights. As this may prompt the former tenant who has paid the sum due under the default notice to apply for an overriding lease[7] the landlord must be sure that he is satisfied with the former tenant's financial standing.[8]

1   *Jervis v Harris* [1995] EGCS 177, CA.
2   The case clarified the uncertainty resulting from conflicting decisions at first instance. In *Swallow Securities v Brand* [1983] 45 P & CR 328, it had been held that a claim for expenses after a landlord had entered and done repairs was covered by the 1938 Act. However, in *Hamilton v Martell Securities* [1984] Ch 266 the court held that the claim was for a debt and the restrictions of the 1938 Act did not apply (followed, by reason of its being the later of two conflicting decisions, in *Colchester Estates v Carlton Industries* [1986] Ch 80 and *Elite Investments v Bainbridge* [1986] 2 EGLR 43).
3   See Appendix 1, Form 1.1, clause 10.4. The advantages of such a clause must be weighed against the potential liability that it creates under the Defective Premises Act 1972, s 4(4), see para 8.29 below.
4   The landlord must be able to recover expenditure incurred as a debt.
5   Either under an authorised guarantee agreement, in the case of a new tenancy, or by virtue of the doctrine of privity of contract, in respect of an old lease.
6   Landlord and Tenant (Covenants) Act 1995, s 17. See para 5.14.1 above.

7   Landlord and Tenant (Covenants) Act 1995, s 19. See para 5.14.2 above.
8   See para 5.14.2 above.

8.24   Amend heading to '*Statutory limitation on damages on termination*'

2   **Add**: *Shortlands Investments Ltd v Cargill plc* [1995] 8 EG 163.

8.27   In the first sentence replace the words 'carry out repairs,' with 'carry out repairs to the property,'.

1   **Add**: There is no requirement to give notice, however, where the landlord's repairing covenant applies, not to the property, but to the building of which it forms part: *British Telecom plc v Sun Life Assurance Society plc* [1995] EGCS 139.

Chapter 9

Landlord's covenants

Add: AA NATURE AND DURATION OF LANDLORD'S COVENANTS

9.1A *Release from covenants on assignment of the reversion.* The Landlord and Tenant (Covenants) Act 1995 has introduced a new regime for landlords' covenants in new tenancies.[1] Under old leases[2] the original landlord remains liable throughout the term of the lease through the doctrine of privity of contract (unless the lease has been drafted so that his liability will end upon assignment). Any subsequent landlords are only liable whilst the reversion is vested in them. However, there is no such distinction under the 1995 Act. When a landlord transfers his interest in a property which is subject to a new tenancy not only will the purchaser become bound by the landlord's covenants with effect from the transfer, but the former landlord will continue to remain liable unless and until he is released from the covenants in accordance with the 1995 Act.[3] This will apply whether or not the landlord is the original landlord who granted the lease

> 1   Landlord and Tenant (Covenants) Act 1995, s 6–8 (inclusive).
> 2   For an explanation of the distinction between old leases and new tenancies for the purpose of the Landlord and Tenant (Covenants) Act 1995, see para 5.11 above.
> 3   Landlord and Tenant (Covenants) Act 1995, s 6.

9.1B *Release under the 1995 Act.*

9.1B.1 *The procedure.* Under the 1995 Act a landlord may apply to be released either wholly or partially from the landlord's covenants when he transfers his interest in the property.[1] The landlord needs to serve notice in the prescribed form[2] on each tenant, requesting a release from the landlord's covenants, not later than four weeks after the transfer.[3] Unless within four weeks after service of the landlord's notice the tenant serves a counter-notice objecting to the release, the landlord will be released to the extent mentioned in his notice.[4] If the tenant serves a counter-notice objecting to the release,[5] the court may, on the landlord's application, and if it is judged reasonable to do so, make an order which has the effect of releasing the landlord to the extent mentioned in his notice.[6] The landlord will remain liable under his covenants if he does not apply for release within the time limit, if he accepts the tenant's objections, or if the court does not declare the release to be reasonable. There will, however, be another opportunity to apply for release when the new landlord (ie the purchaser) disposes of the property.[7]

9.1B.2 *Benefit of tenant's covenants.* If a landlord or former landlord is released from the landlord's covenants, he ceases to be entitled to the benefit of the tenant's covenants.[8] However, the fact that a person ceases to be entitled to the benefit of a covenant does not affect any rights arising from a breach of the covenant occurring before he ceased to be so entitled.[9]

1   Landlord and Tenant (Covenants) Act 1005, s 6
2   For the prescribed forms of notice see 22 *Encyclopaedia of Forms and Precedents* (5th edn) Forms 225.11 – 225.14.
3   Landlord and Tenant (Covenants) Act 1995, s 8(1).
4   Ibid, s 8(2)(a).
5   A tenant may withdraw his objection to the landlord's release at any time, Landlord and Tenant (Covenants) Act 1995, s 8(2)(c).
6   Ibid, s 8(2)(b), (4)(c).
7   In order to protect the landlord's position, should he not be released, the landlord's solicitor should insert in any contract for the sale of the reversion a clause requiring the purchaser to notify the outgoing landlord of the purchaser's own disposal of the property. An express indemnity from the purchaser in respect of the landlord's covenants will also be required.
8   Landlord and Tenant (Covenants) Act, s 6(2)(b) and 7(4).
9   Ibid, s 24(4).

9.1C *Automatic release.* At the time of preparing this Supplement opinion is divided over whether landlords may limit their liability to the period during which they are landlord under the lease. Various devices have been proposed[1] but many commentators believe that any attempt to provide in the lease for an automatic release of the landlord from his liabilities will fall foul of the anti-avoidance provisions contained in the 1995 Act.

1   See the clause for incorporation in a new lease limiting landlord's liability, 22 *Encyclopaedia of Forms and Precedents* (5th edn) Form 225.5. One way of avoiding ongoing liability without contravening the anti-avoidance provisions of the 1995 Act will be to form a management company to become a party to the lease. The company would be liable for matters which would otherwise be landlord's liabilities (for example insurance, structural repair, the provisions of services) and collect the insurance rent and service charge from the tenant. Then when the landlord sells the reversion he can sell the management company with it. Alternatively the landlord might rely on the procedure for release set out in the 1995 Act but introduce an additional tenant's covenant to the effect that the tenant must not unreasonably withhold its consent to a request made by the landlord for a release under the 1995 Act, s 8. This would at least give the landlord a right in damages.

Chapter 10

Insurance

10.15 **Delete** from 'A concern of multiple retailers...' to the end of the paragraph and **replace** with: 'In *Havenbridge Ltd v Boston Dyers Ltd*[2] the tenant covenanted to repay the landlord 'all ... sums as the Landlord shall from time to time properly expend or pay to any insurance company ... for insuring the ... premises'. The landlord claimed £14,000. The tenant suggested that insurance could have been obtained for £3,000, but his argument that a term should be implied to the effect that the insurance costs should be reasonable was rejected. No such term was necessary, nor was it clearly intended although left unexpressed. It was held that 'properly expend or pay' limited the landlord's claim to sums which the landlord had paid or agreed to pay for insurance cover in the ordinary course of business as between the insurer and the landlord. A tenant's challenge will fail if the landlord can show that the premium was negotiated at arm's length and that there were no special factors involved.

2–4 **Delete** entirely and **replace** with:

2 [1994] 49 EG 111. The court followed and approved the reasoning in *Bandar Property Holdings v J S Darwin (Successors) Ltd* [1968] 2 All ER 305. Note too *Serpes Establishments Ltd v KSK Enterprises Ltd* [1993] 2 IR 225, an Irish case, in which it was held that if a tenant can establish that the landlord has clearly gone wrong in an important respect when effecting the insurance cover for which the tenant is ultimately liable, some scope should be allowed for the tenant to dispute the amount. Where the landlord is bona fide and guided by experts, however, the tenant will bear a heavy burden of proof.

Chapter 11

Service charges

Add: **11.4A** *Good practice.* In 1994 the Property Managers Association[1] produced a guide to service charges in commercial leases,[2] the stated aim of which was 'to encourage a good working relationship and to secure co-operation between owners and occupiers through consultation and communication'. In addition to providing helpful guidance on what should and should not be included in service charge costs,[3] the Guide also covers issues such as apportionment, estimated expenditure budgets, certified accounts and sinking funds. Practitioners have not yet taken to citing the Guide in commercial leases but the Guide's influence may yet increase since its use has been encouraged in the more recent 'Code of Practice for Commercial Property Leases in England and Wales'.[4]

1   With support from the Royal Institution of Chartered Surveyors, British Council of Shopping Centres, British Property Federation, British Retail Consortium, Incorporated Society of Valuers and Auctioneers and Shopping Centre Management Group.

2   'Service Charges in Commercial Leases – A Guide to Good Practice', available by post only from The Property Managers Association, c/o Mrs Jill Richardson, Boots the Chemist Ltd, Estates Department, Hargreaves House, Wollaton Street, Nottingham NG1 5FG.

3   See para 11.17, note 2A below.

4   See para 1.6A above.

11.13

1   **Delete** '2.25' and **replace** with '2.24'.
2   **Delete** '2.26' and **replace** with '2.25'.

11.17 **Add**: '2A' after the word 'amounts' in the seventh line of the paragraph.

Add: **2A**   See 'Service Charges in Commercial Leases – A Guide to Good Practice', referred to at para 11.4A above, which recommends that services provided should be 'beneficial and relevant to the needs of the property, the owner, the occupiers and their customers'. The Guide also sets out guidelines as to those items which should be included in service charge costs (including the reasonable costs of maintenance, repair and replacement (where beyond economic repair) of the fabric, plant, equipment and materials necessary for the property; the cost of enhancement of the fabric, plant or equipment where such expenditure can be justified following the analysis of reasonable options and alternatives; and promotional activities) and those that should not be included (eg initial capital costs, setting up costs, capital improvement costs above the costs of normal maintenance, repairs or replacement, future redevelopment costs, and costs between owner and individual occupier arising from enforcement costs for collection of rents, letting costs, various consents, etc).

Chapter 12

Provisos

12.1   **Add** '²ᴬ' after the words 'an action to recover possession' in the fifteenth line of the paragraph.

Add: 2A   The landlord must be sure of his intentions before issuing proceedings. In *GS Fashions Ltd v B & Q plc* [1995] 9 EG 324, following service of a notice under s 146 of the Law of Property Act 1925, the landlord served a writ on the tenant claiming forfeiture on the grounds of breach of the alienation covenant. This was admitted by the tenant in its defence. Subsequently the landlord applied to amend its writ to avoid the forfeiture. The tenant, in turn, sought and obtained a declaration that the lease had been forfeited. The landlord appealed but the court held that service of a writ claiming forfeiture determines the lease and is equivalent to the landlord peaceably re-entering and taking possession, reaffirming the rule in *Associated Deliveries v Harrison* [1984] 272 EG 321. Where a tenant accepts forfeiture of the lease by vacating the premises the landlord will thereupon become liable for the rates, see *Kingston upon Thames Royal London Borough Council v Marlow* [1995] EGCS 161.

Delete: 'branch' in the eighth line and **replace** with 'breach'.

12.3

1   **Add**: See Martin Codd and Terry Bayley, 'The Law of Forfeiture' (1994) New Law Journal 1420 and 1456.

2   **Add**: At the date of preparation of this Supplement the draft Bill is with the Lord Chancellor's Department for consideration.

12.4   **Add**: '⁵ᴬ' after the words 'a break clause.' in the fourth line of this paragraph.

Add: However, the option to determine the lease is often expressed to be personal to the original tenant in order that the right should not pass upon assignment. If this is the intention, the break clause should spell out that the right to break will be extinguished absolutely upon the first assignment.⁷

4   **Add:** See *Willison v Cheverell Estates Ltd* [1995] ECGS 111.

Add: 5A   See Kim Lewison QC and Torquil Gyngell, 'Tenants' Break Clauses: When and how to use them' (The Blundell Memorial Lecture 1995) for a thorough and informed view.

Add: 7   See *Olympia & York Canary Wharf Ltd v Oil Property Investments Ltd* [1994] EGLR 48; and *Max Factor Ltd v Wesleyan Assurance Society* [1995] 41 EG 146 in which Max Factor was granted a 25 year lease which contained a mutual right to break, expressed to be personal to Max Factor, exercisable at the end of the tenth year. Max Factor assigned the lease but, a year later, it was assigned back and Max Factor subsequently sought to operate the break clause. The landlord contended that the right to break had been lost upon first assignment – it was not available to Max Factor as reassignee. The court found in favour of the landlord, ruling that the right to break had been limited to the period during which Max Factor was the original tenant. Whilst this may support the parties' likely intention when the lease was first drafted, the court's construction of the actual wording of the break clause was certainly generous to the landlord.

12.5   **Add**: It is also recommended that tenants ensure that the break clause specify the date upon which notice to determine should be given and the date upon which it will expire.[8]

1   **Add** after the references for *Bairstow Eves*: *Trane (UK) Ltd v Provident Mutual Life Assurance* [1995] 3 EG 122.
         Add: after *Robinson v Thames Mead Estates Ltd*: and *Bass Holdings Ltd v Morton Music Ltd* [1987] 2 All ER 1001, CA.

3   **Add**: Somewhat surprisingly, given the errors contained in the notice, *Carradine* (see above) was followed in *Micrografix v Woking 8 Ltd* [1995] 37 EG 179. However, *Hankey* (see above) was followed by the Court of Appeal in *Mannai Investment Co Ltd v Eagle Star Life Assurance Co Ltd* [1995] EGCS 124 where a notice was held to be invalid that referred to 12 January when the correct date was 13 January. In *Trane (UK) Ltd v Provident Mutual Life Assurance* [1995] 3 EG 122 the tenant served notice by reference to the date of the lease rather than the commencement date of the term and the notice was therefore held to be invalid. See also *A & J Mucklow (Birmingham) Ltd v Metro-Cammell Weymann Ltd* [1994] EGCS 64.

Add: 8   See *Trane* (referred to at note 3 above) and *Meadfield Properties Ltd v Secretary of State for the Environment* [1994] EGCS 144.

12.7   **Add:** A new Arbitration Bill was introduced into the House of Lords in December 1995. Under the terms of the new Bill, which is intended to strengthen the current law, the powers of arbitrators will be enhanced and unnecessary intervention by the courts in the arbitral process will be curtailed. A court will be able to act in support of the arbitration only when the arbitral tribunal is unable to act itself.

Chapter 13

Underleases

13.2   In the seventeenth line of the paragraph, **insert** '⁴ᴬ' after the words 'superior landlord'.

1   **Add** after the words 'given to it' in the third line of the footnote: 'under s 6 of the Law of Distress Amendment Act 1908'.

Add: 4A   By virtue of the Landlord and Tenant (Covenants) Act 1995 a superior landlord may only require a sublessee to covenant for the period during which the sublessee is bound by the tenant's covenants contained in the underlease and for any period during which it is liable under an authorised guarantee agreement. See para 7.1.5 above.

13.3.4 Add after the word 'leases' in the second line the words 'which are not new tenancies for the purpose of the Landlord and Tenant (Covenants) Act 1995'.

4   **Amend** 'para 5.12.5' to 'para 5.12'.

13.11

2   **Delete** 'see para 5.12, note 5 above' and **replace** with: see *Monkland v Jack Barclay Ltd* [1951] 2 KB 252, [1951] 1 All ER 714, CA; *Terrell v Mabie Todd & Co Ltd* [1952] 2 TLR 574; *Lipmans Wallpaper Ltd v Mason & Hodghton Ltd* [1969] 1 Ch 20, [1968] 1 All ER 1123; *NW Investments (Erdington) Ltd v Swani* (1970) 214 Estates Gazette 1115; *Bickel v Courtenay Investments (Nominees) Ltd* [1984] 1 All ER 657, [1984] 1 WLR 795. In the light of *IBM United Kingdom Ltd v Rockware Glass Ltd* [1980] FSR 335, CA, it may be that there is little practical difference between a covenant to use best endeavours, a covenant to use reasonable endeavours and a covenant to take all reasonable steps. See also *UBH (Mechanical Services) Ltd v Standard Life Assurance Co* (1986) Times, 13 November; *Agroexport State Enterprise for Foreign Trade v Cie Européenne de Céreales* [1974] 1 Lloyd's Rep 499; *R v East Hertfordshire District Council, ex p Dalhold Resources Management (UK) Pty Ltd* (189) 22 HLR 77, [1990] 1 EGLR 12; *P & O Property Holdings Ltd v Norwich Union Life Insurance Society* [1993] EGCS 69, CA.

13.12

3   **Add:** The service of a notice to quit by a tenant to his landlord will determine the sub-tenancy, because this falls within the general rule that a subtenancy perishes with the tenancy that supports it: *Pennell v Payne* [1995] QB 192, [1995] 06 EG 152, CA, discussed at [1995] 08 EG 162. See also G Fife, 'Termination of Leases', 41 EG 134.

Chapter 14

Renewal of business leases

14.3

2   **Add**: *Esso Petroleum Co Ltd v Fumegrange Ltd* [1994] 2 EGLR 90, [1994] 46 EG 199, CA.

5   **Add:** See *Graysim Holdings Ltd v P & O Property Holdings Ltd* [1996] 1 AC 329, [1996] 03 EG 124, HL which concerned a covered market where the tenant had sub-let stalls to individual traders. Each sub-tenant had exclusive possession of his stall but the tenant retained the common parts and provided services through a full time manager of the property. Overturning the trial judge, the Court of Appeal held the tenant to have 'sufficient presence and control' to amount to business occupation of the whole of the property. This caused grave consternation amongst headlandlords since it raised the possibility of tenant and sub-tenant enjoying statutory protection in respect of the same premises (and, therefore, both being entitled to statutory compensation). To the relief of headlandlords, however, the House of Lords restored the trial judge's ruling, closing the door on the possibility of dual occupation entitling both tenant and sub-tenant to statutory protection.

7   **Extend** last sentence by adding: and the 1954 Act does not cease to apply to a tenancy where the tenant vacates before the expiry of the contractual term and thus the tenant still has to serve a notice under the 1954 Act, s 27: *Esselte AB v Pearl Assurance plc* [1995] 2 EGLR 61, [1995] 37 EG 173, see para 14.17 below.

14.5

2   **Add:** In *Nicholls v Kinsey* [1994] 1 EGLR 131, [1994] 16 EG 145 a tenancy was expressed to be for a period of 12 months and to continue thereafter from year to year terminable by the landlord giving 12 months notice. An order had been obtained excluding the 1954 Act but the Court of Appeal held that the prospective tenancy was not for a term of years certain and as such, there could be no authorisation because the jurisdiction of the County Court is exclusively statutory and any departure from s 38 renders the authorisation invalid. Thus the 1954 Act applied to the tenancy because the attempt to exclude it had been ineffective.

5   **Add:** As to the appropriate rent payable by a tenant holding over after the expiry of a lease where the 1954 Act does not apply, see *Dean & Chapter of the Cathedral & Metropolitan Church of Christ, Canterbury v Whitbread plc* [1995] 1 EGLR 82, [1995] 24 EG. 148.

14.7   Add: '9' to the end of paragraph (d).

3   **Add:** As to the effect of a misleading notice see *M & P Enterprises (London) Ltd v Norfolk Square Hotels Ltd* [1994] 1 EGLR 129, [1994] 14 EG 128.

4   **Add:** See also *Gudka v Patel & Others* (1994) unreported, CA (but see Comm.Leases 1995, 9(2)).

14.14   Add: Where a landlord exercises a right of early determination, he will not be able to invoke the provisions of a rent review clause contained in the lease during any period of statutory continuation under the 1954 Act unless the expression 'the term' was defined in the lease as including any statutory continuation of it.[12]

Add: 12   See *Willison v Cheverell Estates Ltd & Another* [1995] EGCS 111, CA where premises were demised for a term of 20 years, subject to earlier determination by the landlord for demolition or reconstruction. The lease was subject to five year upwards only rent reviews. The landlord gave six months' notice to the tenant, pursuant to the terms of the lease, determining the term after 9½ years. The second review date fell subsequent to the expiration of the notice determining the term. The Court of Appeal held that the 1954 Act drew a clear distinction between the original contractual term and the statutory estate that followed. The break clause notice was effective to cut down the term demised to the date of expiry of the notice and there was therefore no longer any term after that date in respect of which the rent review provision could be invoked. It was the tenancy and not the term that was continued under the 1954 Act.

14.17   **Add:** In *Esselte AB v Pearl Assurance plc*,[8] the tenant claimed that the 1954 Act had ceased to apply by the expiry of the contractual term because the tenant had vacated the property, and was thus not occupying it for the purposes of a business.[9] Accordingly, the tenant argued, the tenancy terminated on the contractual expiry date, and so no notice was required under s 27. It was held, however, that once a tenancy had been caught by the 1954 Act, the Act continues to apply to any continuation of that tenancy and thus a notice under s 27 is required to terminate the tenancy. This approach is unexceptional to the extent that it applies to those cases where a tenant ceases to be in business occupation shortly before the contractual expiry date, but it could cause uncertainty if it is intended to apply where the tenant has long since given up business occupation, and especially where there has been a subsequent business occupier.[10]

8   [1995] 2 EGLR 61, [1995] 37 EG 173.
9   See 1954 Act, s 23(1), para 14.3 above.
10   See K Lewison QC 'Ruling on ending tenancy is terminally problematic' [1995] Property Week 3/10 August. Does the decision in *Esselte AB* mean that a tenant who has occupied property for its business, then sub-let the whole, will still have to serve a Section 27 Notice even if the sub-tenant's tenancy is being renewed under the 1954 Act? If so, this would seem inconsistent with the House of Lords' decision in *Graysim Holdings Ltd v P & O Property Holdings Ltd* [1996] 1 AC 329, [1996] 03 EG 124, see para 14.3 above. The decision in *Esselte AB* also raises the question of whether landlords should serve a Section 25 Notice on any tenant who has previously been in business occupation of the property. At the date of this Supplement the case is due to be appealed to the Court of Appeal, which will no doubt have regard to its earlier decision in *Long Acre Securities Limited* (see Note 3 above). It is to be hoped that the decision on appeal will clarify the present confusion.

14.28 **Delete** last sentence and **replace** with: 'This method, however, may impose upon the tenant liability pursuant to the terms of an authorised guarantee agreement[7] and is unlikely to be an attractive proposition to him.'

Delete '7' at the end of the final sentence.

7   **Delete** entirely and **replace** with: 7 See para 5.13.2 above.

14.29

5   **Add**: It appears that the landlord may vary the offer of alternative accommodation between the service of the s 25 notice and the hearing: *Chaplin Ltd v Regent Capital Holdings Ltd* [1994] 1 EGLR 249.

14.31

5   **Add**: *Turner v Wandsworth LBC* (1994) 69 P & CR 433, [1994] 25 EG 148

14.40

3   **Add:** For the purpose of calculating compensation the rateable value or business rate to be multiplied by the appropriate multiplier is determined by reference to the date of service of the landlord's Section 25 Notice (*Brewer v Vesco* (1994) unreported, CA (but see Comm.Leases 1994, 8(11))).

6   **Add** new reference for: *Busby v Co-operative Insurance Society Ltd* [1994] 1 EGLR 136, [1994] 06 EG 141.

14.45

2   **Add:** For new tenancies, which will be subject to the Landlord and Tenant (Covenants) Act 1995, the distinction between covenants which 'touch and concern' the land and those which do not is abolished; s 2 of the 1995 Act. The 1995 Act provides that the benefit and burden of all landlord and tenant covenants of a tenancy shall be annexed and incident to the premises and of the reversion in them and shall pass on an assignment of the premises or the reversion in them.

14.47

4   **Add:** *Rumbelows Ltd v Tameside MBC* (1994) unreported (but see [1995] 14 EG 132), *Merseyside Glass Ltd v J D Williams* (1994) unreported (but see [1995] 14 EG 132), and *Ganton House Investments Ltd v Crossman Investments Ltd* [1993] unreported (but see [1994] 15 EG 154).

14.50 Add: After 1 January 1996 the matters which are to be taken into account by the court in determining the rent will include any effect on rent of the operation of the provisions of the Landlord and Tenant (Covenants) Act 1995.[8]

Add: 8   Ibid, s 34(4) as inserted by the Landlord and Tenant (Covenants) Act 1995 s 30(1), Schedule 1, para 3.

14.51

1   **Replace** the first part of this footnote with the following: The usual rules of evidence apply. In the past there has been no principle permitting hearsay in relation to comparable transactions: *English Exporters (London) Ltd v Eldonwall Ltd* [1973] Ch 415, [1973] 1 All ER 726; and *Rogers v Rosedimond Investments (Blakes Market) Ltd* (1978) 247 Estates Gazette 467, CA; *Town Centre Securities Ltd v Wm Morrison Supermarkets Ltd* (1981) 263 Estates Gazette 435. However, the Civil Evidence Act 1995 (which received Royal Assent on 8 November 1995, but will only come into force on the making of the necessary commencement orders) will provide that in civil proceedings, evidence shall not be excluded on the ground that it is hearsay. Civil proceedings are defined in the Act as 'proceedings, before any tribunal, in which the strict rules of evidence apply, whether as a matter of strict law or by agreement of the parties'. At the present time there seems some uncertainty as to what effect this piece of legislation will have on the common direction by arbitrators excluding hearsay evidence of comparables in determining rent review. As to comments on valuation generally ... (continue to the end of the footnote).

14.53

6   **Extend** the last sentence by adding: , where a 2.5% uplift in rent was given to compensate the landlord for an upwards and downwards rent review clause. However, no such uplift was given in *Forbuoys plc v Newport BC* [1994] 1 EGLR 13, [1994] 24 EG 156, where an upwards/downwards clause was ordered. For an example of a case

where the lease being renewed contained an upwards only clause see *Charles Follett Ltd v Cabtell Investments Ltd* [1986] 2 EGLR 76; 280 Estates Gazette 639. In that case the High Court refused to modify the existing clause in order to permit the new clause to operate a downwards review.

Add: **14.59A** *The effect of the Landlord and Tenant (Covenants) Act 1995.* Renewal leases which are granted under the 1954 Act after 1 January 1996 will be new tenancies for the purposes of the Landlord and Tenant (Covenants) Act 1995.[1] The 1954 Act is amended[2] so that, in determining the rent and terms of the tenancy on renewal, the court should take into account the effect of the Landlord and Tenant (Covenants) Act 1995. Any amendments to the terms of the tenancy, particularly with regard to the alienation provisions, will be considered not only by reference to *O'May* but also in the light of the changes introduced by the 1995 Act. It is difficult to predict the way in which the courts will interpret the new directions but it must be expected that changes will be permitted to the terms of a tenancy to reflect the automatic release of tenants from their covenants[3] and the ability of landlords to require outgoing tenants on assignment to enter into authorised guarantee agreements.[4] Landlords will presumably argue for the right to agree in advance the terms upon which consent to assignment may be given.[5] In determining the rent the court will need to have regard to the valuation consequences of the provisions of the 1995 Act and any resultant changes to the terms of the tenancy.

1   For the distinction between old leases, in respect of which the original contracting parties will continue to remain liable throughout the term of the lease, and new tenancies which will be subject to the Landlord and Tenant (Covenants) Act 1995, see para 5.11 above.
2   See 1954 Act, s 34(4) as inserted by the Landlord and Tenant (Covenants) Act 1995, s 30(1), Schedule 1, para 3; and the 1954 Act, s 35(2) as inserted by the Landlord and Tenant (Covenants) Act s 30(1), Schedule 1, para 4.
3   See para 5.13 above.
4   See para 5.13.2 above.
5   See para 7.5A above.

Chapter 15

After the lease has been agreed

15.4 **Add** the word 'against' after the words 'the third-party tenant but not' in the second line.

15.5 In the second sentence, **delete** the words 'The receiver may not be appointed' and **replace** with the words 'The power of appointing should not be exercised'.

In the tenth line, **delete** the words 'be made a party to' and **replace** with the words 'join into'.

15.6 In the fourth line **replace** the words 'and the corporate seal attested' with the words 'and if the corporate seal is used it should be attested'.

15.9 In the fifth line, after the words 'have been obtained', **insert**: Recently there seems to have been an increase in the number of side letters that are exchanged on completion of the granting of a lease. These are prompted by a number of factors, for example, a one-off concession to the original tenant or perhaps some term that the landlord might prefer was not obvious if that transaction was ever used as a comparable on another letting. The drafting of any side letter must leave no doubt as to whether the successors of the two original parties are to be bound.[3A]

Add: 3A *System Floors Ltd v Ruralpride Ltd* [1995] 1 EGLR 48, [1995] 07 EG 125, CA (discussed at 124). See also *Lotteryking Ltd v AMEC Properties Ltd* [1995] 28 EG 104 in which it was held that a side letter entered into prior to the grant of a lease (but called into scrutiny after the lease had been granted), under which the landlord had agreed to carry out repairs, did not fall foul of the Law of Property (Miscellaneous Provisions) Act 1989, s 2 and, since it 'touched and concerned' the land, bound successors in title of the landlord.

15.10 **Replace** the second sentence with: The duty is ad valorem on the amount of the premium and the amount of the rent[2] which will depend upon the length of the term.[3]

In the third sentence **delete** the words ', or, in the rare instances when the duty on the lease is less than 50p, the same duty as is payable on the lease.'[4] **Renumber** the remaining footnote references within the paragraph.

Replace the penultimate sentence of the paragraph with: Furthermore, failure to stamp a lease within 30 days will mean that the tenant will have to pay a fine, a penalty and interest.

Add to the end of the paragraph: Although stamp duty is normally paid post-completion, it needs to be considered during the planning stage of any transaction to avoid any unnecessary payment of duty.

1   After the words 'As to the rates of duty' **insert** the words 'on the rent'. **Amend** 'Finance Act 1980, s 128' to 'Finance Act 1980, s 95, Finance Act 1982, s 128.

2   In the fifth line **replace** the word 'rent' with the word 'charges'.
      Replace the last two lines with the words 'provisions where both (i) the occupation rent does not exceed £600.00 per annum; and (ii) the premium paid does not exceed £60,000'.

4   **Delete** entirely.

5–13   **Renumber** 4 to 12.

14   **Renumber** as **13** and **replace** the text with: See Inland Revenue Statement of Practice (SP11/91) 12 September 1991 and Guidance Note issued by the Institute of Chartered Accountants (Tax 19/92 Guidance Note) and paras 2.22 – 2.26 above.

Appendix 1

Precedents

FORM 1.1   LEASE OF WHOLE BUILDING: LONG FORM

CONTENTS

Add: 10.18   Consent to Landlord's release
Add: Schedule 1   Authorised guarantee agreement.

9. Alienation

Replace clauses 9.1–9.9 with the following:

9.1   *Definitions*

In this Lease:

9.1.1   "Application" means an application from the Tenant for the Landlord's consent to the Proposed Assignment

9.1.2   "Authorised Guarantee Agreement"[80a] means a deed in the form set out in Schedule 1 with such amendments (if any) as the Landlord reasonably requires[80b] and being an authorised guarantee agreement as defined in the 1995 Act, section 16

9.1.3   "Current Tenant" means the person in whom the Term is vested at the date of the Application

9.1.4   "Proposed Assignee" means the person stated in the Application to whom the Current Tenant wishes to assign this Lease

9.1.5   "Proposed Assignment" means a proposed assignment of the Property by the Current Tenant to the Proposed Assignee for which the Landlord's consent is requested in the Application

9.1.6   "Proposed Guarantor" means the person or persons (if any) who must not be or include the Current Tenant stated in the Application who it is proposed will guarantee to the Landlord the obligations of the Proposed Assignee

9.2 *General covenants*

The Tenant covenants with the Landlord:

9.2.1   except to the extent permitted under the subsequent provisions of this clause not to:

- part with possession of the Property or any part of it
- permit another to occupy the Property or any part of it

- share the occupation of the Property or any part of it
- hold the Property or any part of it on trust for another

but the Tenant may allow a company that is a member of the same group as the Tenant (within the meaning of the 1954 Act, section 42) to occupy the whole or part of the Property for so long as both companies remain members of the same group and otherwise than in a manner that transfers or creates a legal estate

9.2.2   not to assign underlet or charge part[81] only of the Property

9.2.3   not to assign the whole of the Property without the consent of the Landlord (such consent not to be unreasonably withheld) provided that the Landlord shall be entitled (for the purposes of section 19(1A) of the Landlord and Tenant Act 1927):

9.2.3.1   to withhold its consent in any of the circumstances set out in clause 9.3.1 and

9.2.3.2   to impose all or any of the matters set out in clause 9.3.2 as a condition of its consent

and the provisos to this clause 9.2.3 shall operate without prejudice to the right of the Landlord to withhold such consent on any other ground or grounds where such withholding of consent would be reasonable or to impose any further condition or conditions upon the grant of consent where the imposition of such consent or consents would be reasonable[80c]

9.2.4   not to underlet the whole of the Property without the consent of the Landlord such consent not to be unreasonably withheld where the Tenant has complied with the provisions of clause 9.5[82]

9.2.5   not to charge the whole of the Property without the consent of the Landlord such consent not to be unreasonably withheld

9.3   *Circumstances and conditions*[80d]

9.3.1   The circumstances referred to in clause 9.2.3.1 are:

9.3.1.1   Where in the reasonable opinion of the Landlord the Proposed Assignee is not of sufficient financial standing to enable it to comply with the Tenant's covenants and conditions contained in this Lease throughout the Term

[9.3.1.2   Where the Proposed Assignee is an associated company of the Current Tenant[80e]

9.3.1.3   Where in the reasonable opinion of the Landlord the value of the Landlord's interest in the Property would be diminished or otherwise adversely affected by the Proposed Assignment on the assumption (whether or not a fact) that the Landlord wished to sell its interest the day following completion of the Proposed Assignment of this Lease to the Proposed Assignee;

9.3.1.4   Where the Proposed Assignee enjoys diplomatic or state immunity [but this circumstance shall not apply where the Proposed Assignee is the Government of the United Kingdom of Great Britain and Northern Ireland or any department thereof]

9.3.1.5   Where the Proposed Assignee is not resident [in the EC] [in a jurisdiction where reciprocal enforcement of judgments exists]]

9.3.2   The conditions referred to in clause 9.2.3.2 are:

9.3.2.1   The execution and delivery to the Landlord prior to completion of the Proposed Assignment of an Authorised Guarantee Agreement

9.3.2.2   The payment to the Landlord of all rents and other sums which have fallen due under this Lease prior to the date of the Proposed Assignment

[9.3.2.3   The provision of any requisite consent of any superior landlord or mortgagee and confirmation that any lawfully imposed condition of such consent has been satisfied[80f]

9.3.2.4   On a Proposed Assignment to a Limited Company the execution and delivery to the Landlord by the Proposed Guarantor prior to the Proposed Assignment of a deed of covenant guaranteeing the performance of the Proposed Assignee [in the form of clauses 19.1–19.3 or] in such [other] form as the Landlord reasonably requires[80b]

9.3.2.5   The execution and delivery to the Landlord prior to the Proposed Assignment of a rent deposit deed for such sum as the Landlord may reasonably determine in such form as the Landlord may reasonably require together with the payment by way of cleared funds of the sum specified in the rent deposit deed

9.3.2.6   The Application is accompanied by:

• certified copies of the Proposed Assignee's or Proposed Guarantor's audited accounts for each of the three financial years immediately preceding the date of the Application
• references from:
– the Proposed Assignee's or Proposed Guarantor's bankers confirming that the Proposed Assignee or Proposed Guarantor is considered good for the rents payable under this Lease and
– if the Proposed Assignee or Proposed Guarantor is a lessee of other premises at least one of its lessors confirming that the Proposed Assignee or Proposed Guarantor has been a satisfactory lessee and
[• an undertaking from Solicitors acting for the Current Tenant or for the Proposed Assignee or Proposed Guarantor to pay all costs disbursements and any VAT thereon which may be properly incurred by the Landlord in considering the Application whether or not consent is granted and in granting consent (if it is granted)]]

9.3.2.7   If at any time prior to the Proposed Assignment taking place the circumstances (or any of them) specified in clause 9.3.1 apply the Landlord may revoke its consent to the Proposed Assignment by written notice to the Tenant.

9.4   *Determinations*

9.4.1   Any question of whether or not any of the circumstances set out in clause 9.3.1 apply in relation to the Proposed Assignment or as to whether any of the conditions referred to in clause 9.3.2 should be imposed shall be determined by the Landlord and if the Landlord determines that any of the circumstances apply or that any of the conditions should be imposed the Landlord must give written notice to that effect to the Tenant and such notification will be binding on the Tenant unless within 14 days of the service of the notice the Tenant serves on the Landlord a counternotice ("Counternotice") requiring the Landlord's determination to be reviewed by a third party in accordance with clause 9.4.2

9.4.2   If a Counternotice is served the Landlord's determination shall be reviewed by an independent third party acting as an expert and not as an arbitrator who shall be agreed or appointed in accordance with clause 9.4.3 and whose decision shall be conclusive and binding

9.4.3   The third party must be a Chartered Surveyor with not less than ten years' post qualification experience appointed by agreement between the Landlord and the Tenant or in the absence of such agreement nominated at the request of either of them by the President for the time being of The Royal Institution of Chartered Surveyors (or his duly appointed deputy or anyone authorised by him to make appointments on his behalf)

9.4.4   The fees payable to the President or any such third party shall be borne and paid by the Landlord and the Tenant in such shares and in such manner as the third party shall determine and failing any such decision in equal shares (and if one party shall pay all the fees it shall be entitled to recover from the other any appropriate share which is due)

9.5   Underletting

9.5.1   Any consent of the Landlord to an underletting of the whole of the Property will be subject to conditions that:[82]

9.5.1.1   the undertenant enters into a deed with the Landlord in which the undertenant covenants that during the period when the undertenant is bound by the tenant covenants contained in the underlease together with any additional period during which the undertenant is bound by an authorised guarantee agreement the undertenant will observe and perform the provisions of this Lease (excluding the covenant as to the payment of rent) and the provisions of the underlease[83]

9.5.1.2   the underlease is granted without a fine or premium at a rent no lower than the then open market rent approved by the Landlord (such approval not to be unreasonably withheld)[85]

9.5.1.3   the rent is payable in advance on the same days as rent is payable under this Lease

9.5.1.4   the underlease contains provisions approved by the Landlord (such approval not to be unreasonably withheld):

- for the upwards-only review of the rent on the basis set out in clause 4 or in such other form as the Landlord reasonably requires or approves
- for the rent to be reviewed either on the Review Dates or on such other dates approved by the Landlord by which the rent is reviewed no less frequently
- prohibiting the undertenant from doing or allowing any act or thing in relation to the Property inconsistent with or in breach of the provisions of this Lease

- for re-entry by the underlandlord on breach of any covenant by the undertenant
- imposing an absolute prohibition against all dealings with the Property other than an assignment or charge of the whole
- prohibiting any assignment of the whole of the Property without the consent of the Landlord under this Lease and except on the basis set out in clauses 9.1–9.5 of this Lease such provisions being incorporated into the underlease
- prohibiting any charge of the whole of the Property without the consent of the Landlord under this Lease
- prohibiting the undertenant from parting with possession or permitting another to share or occupy or hold on trust for another the Property or any part of it
- imposing in relation to any permitted assignment the same obligations for registration with the Landlord as are in this Lease in relation to dispositions by the Tenant
- excluding the provisions of the 1954 Act, sections 24–28 from the letting created by the underlease[86]

9.5.2   The Tenant covenants with the Landlord:

9.5.2.1   to enforce the performance by every undertenant of the provisions of the underlease and not at any time to waive any breach of the covenants or conditions on the part of any undertenant or assignee of any underlease nor (without the consent of the Landlord such consent not to be unreasonably withheld) to vary the terms of any underlease

9.5.2.2   not to agree any reviewed rent with the undertenant without the approval of the Landlord such approval not to be unreasonably withheld

9.5.2.3   not to agree any appointment of a person as the third party determining the revised rent without the approval of the Landlord such approval not to be unreasonably withheld

9.5.2.4   to incorporate as part of its representations to that third party representations required by the Landlord

9.5.2.5   to give the Landlord details of every rent review within twenty-eight days of its outcome

9.5.2.6   not to grant the underlease or permit the undertenant to occupy the Property unless an order has been obtained under the 1954 Act, section 38(4)[86]

9.5.2.7   not to accept the surrender of or forfeit or otherwise determine any underlease without the consent of the Landlord

9.6   *Insolvency of covenantors*

The Tenant covenants with the Landlord:

9.6.1   to give notice to the Landlord within fourteen days if any person who has entered into covenants with the Landlord under the provisions of this clause (where that person has not been released from these obligations) becomes Insolvent (as defined in clause 13.2) or dies

9.6.2   if requested by the Landlord following the service of a notice under clause 9.6.1 to procure that within 14 days of the request some other person reasonably acceptable to the Landlord enters into covenants with the Landlord in substantially the same form

9.7   *Notice to the Landlord of alienation*

Within twenty-one days of any assignment charge underlease or any transmission or other devolution relating to the Property the Tenant covenants with the Landlord to produce for registration with the Landlord's solicitor a certified copy of any relevant document and to pay the Landlord's solicitor's reasonable charge for registration of at least £25

10. Tenant's other covenants

Add after clause 10.6.3 the following:

10.6.4   without prejudice to the generality of the above:

10.6.4.1   to comply at the Tenant's expense with the Construction (Design and Management) Regulations 1994 ("CDM Regulations") and to be the only client (as defined in the CDM Regulations) and to fulfil in relation to all and any works all the obligations of the client as set out in or reasonably to be inferred from the CDM Regulations and to make a declaration to that effect[94a] to the Health and Safety Executive in accordance with the Approved Code of Practice publicised from time to time by the Health and Safety Commission in relation to the CDM Regulations and the provisions of clause 12.2.9 shall apply to these obligations and

10.6.4.2   at the end of the Term forthwith to deliver to the Landlord any and all health and safety files relating to the Property in accordance with the CDM Regulations

10.18   *Consent to Landlord's release*

not to unreasonably withhold consent to a request made by the Landlord under the 1995 Act, section 8 for a release from the landlord covenants of this Lease

11. Landlord's covenants

Replace heading with: **11. Landlord's covenants**[102a].

16. Interpretation

In clause 16.3 **add** footnote '142a' after the word 'end'.

Renumber clause 16.7 as '16.7.1' and **add**: '16.7.2   "1995 Act" means the Landlord and Tenant (Covenants) Act 1995'.

Replace clause 16.13 with the following:

16.13   "Tenant" means any person bound by the tenant covenants of this Lease from time to time

16.13.1   the person from time to time in whom the tenant's interest under this Lease is vested and

16.13.2   any person in whom the tenant's interest under this Lease had been vested and who has not been released by the 1995 Act

19. Guarantor

Insert the following immediately after the heading:

19.1   The Guarantor's covenants with the Landlord are as sole or principal debtor or covenantor with the Landlord for the time being and with all of its successors in title (without the need for any express assignment[153]) so that the Guarantor's obligations to the Landlord will last:

19.1.1   while the Tenant is bound by the tenant's covenants under this lease[152a] and

19.1.2   for any period during which the Tenant shall be liable under any Authorised Guarantee Agreement required by the Landlord pursuant to clause 9.3[152b]

Renumber clauses 19.1–19.3.2 as 19.2–19.4.2 and **renumber** references to those clauses in the text.

In clause 19.2 (as renumbered) **replace** the words 'The Guarantor . . . in title:' with the words 'The Guarantor covenants:'.

SCHEDULE 1

After the words '[163] [WE CERTIFY . . . gives effect][164] **insert** Schedule 1 as follows:

SCHEDULE 1

DATED _____ 199___

and

_____

AUTHORISED GUARANTEE AGREEMENT[164]

[address of the Property]
_____

[Name of Landlord's Solicitors]
[Address:

                                                    ]

Tel: [   ]
Fax: [   ]
Ref: [   ]

AUTHORISED GUARANTEE AGREEMENT

DATE: 199

PARTIES:

(1)   [   ] of [
                            ] ("Landlord") and
(2)   [   ] of [
                            ] ("Tenant")

1. Definitions and recitals

1.1   This Deed is supplemental to a lease [an underlease] ("the Lease") dated
the [   ] and made between (1) [the Landlord] and (2) [the Tenant] by
which the property known as [   ] ("the Property") was demised for a
term of [   ] years from [and including] the [   ] ("the Term") subject
to the payment of the rent [s] reserved by and the performance of the provisions
of the Lease

1.2   The reversion immediately expectant on the determination of the Term [remains *or* is now] vested in the Landlord and the unexpired residue of the Term [remains *or* is now] vested in the Tenant

1.3   The Lease contains provisions prohibiting the Tenant from assigning the Property without the consent of the Landlord such consent not to be unreasonably withheld in certain circumstances and further provides that any consent will be subject to a condition that the Tenant enters into an authorised guarantee agreement as defined in the Landlord and Tenant (Covenants) Act 1995 ("the 1995 Act")

1.4   The Landlord has agreed (at the request of the Tenant) to grant a licence to the Tenant to assign its estate and interest in the Property to [   ] of [   ] ("Assignee") subject to the Tenant and the Assignee entering into a formal licence in the form required by the Landlord and the Tenant entering into this Authorised Guarantee Agreement

1.5   All terms defined in the Lease have the same meanings when used in this deed except where the contrary appears

2. Authorised Guarantee Agreement

2.1   This Deed is an authorised guarantee agreement as defined in the 1995 Act, section 16

2.2   Nothing in this Deed imposes on the Tenant:

- any requirement to guarantee the performance under the Lease of any person other than the Assignee or
- any liability restriction or other requirement (of whatever nature) in relation to any time after the Assignee is released by the Act from its obligations under the Lease

3. Tenant's covenants[165]

The Tenant covenants with the Landlord and (without the need for any express assignment) with all of its successors in title:

3.1   if the Assignee does not pay the Rent or any other sum due under the Lease on the date on which it is due to pay to the Landlord on demand the Rent or other sum

3.2   if the Assignee is in breach of any provision of the Lease to remedy that breach on demand and to indemnify and keep indemnified the Landlord against all Losses suffered by the Landlord as a result (directly or indirectly) of that breach

3.3   in addition to the obligations set out in clauses 3.1 and 3.2 and if the Lease is disclaimed by the Assignee's trustee in bankruptcy or liquidator:

3.3.1   to pay to the Landlord on demand an amount equal to the Rent and other sums of a recurring nature that would have been payable under the Lease for the period beginning on the date of disclaimer and ending on the earliest of:

- the date upon which the Property is re-let
- the expiry of the Term
- the expiry of the period of [one year] beginning on the date of the disclaimer[166] or

3.3.2   if requested by the Landlord within ninety days of disclaimer to take from the Landlord a lease of the Property from the date of disclaimer for the residue of the Term at the Rent payable at the time of disclaimer or (where a rent review is pending at the time of disclaimer at the Rent that is subsequently agreed or determined under clause 4 of the Lease to have been payable at the time of disclaimer) and upon the same terms as those contained in the Lease with all provisions of a periodical nature (including for example those relating to review of the Rent) expressed to apply on the actual dates that would have applied if the Lease had not been disclaimed and

3.3.3   to pay the costs of the Landlord incurred in relation to the disclaimer and where appropriate the grant of the lease to the Tenant

4. Application of Tenant's covenants

The obligations of the Tenant set out in clause 3 will continue to apply even if:

4.1   the Landlord grants any time or indulgence to the Assignee or fails to enforce payment of the Rent or any other sum or the performance of the terms of the Lease

4.2   the Landlord refuses to accept the Rent tendered when the Landlord was entitled (or would after the service of a notice under the Law of Property Act 1925, section 146 be entitled) to re-enter the Property

4.3   the terms of the Lease are varied except where the variation is a relevant variation as defined in the 1995 Act, section 18 (4)

4.4   a revised Rent has been agreed or determined under clause 4 of the Lease [including any stepped rent phased rent or other rental formula that may be agreed][167]

4.5   the Assignee surrenders part of the Demised Premises and where this happens the liability of the Tenant under the Lease continues for the part of the Demised Premises not surrendered after making any necessary apportionments under the Law of Property Act 1925, section 140

4.6   the Tenant would have been released by any other event

5. Duration of the Tenant's covenant

[5.1]   The obligations of the Tenant set out in clause 3 above apply for the period beginning on the date upon which the Property is assigned to the Assignee and ending on the date upon which the Assignee is released by the Act from its obligations under the Lease

[5.2   The Landlord covenants with the Tenant that it will notify the Tenant in writing within [   ] days of the Assignee being released by the 1995 Act from its obligations under the Lease[168]]

[6. Recovery of Payments

6.1   The Landlord covenants that before attempting to recover any such payment as is described in clause 6.2 from the Tenant it will serve on the Tenant a notice as if that payment was a fixed charge under the 1995 Act[169]

6.2   The payment referred to in clause 6.1 is any amount payable in respect of any breach of covenant by the Assignee which:

6.2.1   has been finally determined by a court or in binding arbitration; or

6.2.2   has been agreed between the Landlord and the Assignee

6.3   The notice in respect of the payments referred to in clause 6.2 shall be in the form prescribed by section 27 of the 1995 Act with such variations as may be appropriate to the circumstances

6.4   The Tenant shall not be liable for any of the payments referred to in clause 6.2 unless within the period of six months of the payment being determined or agreed the Landlord serves on the Tenant a notice under this clause]

SIGNED as a deed but not	)
delivered until the date of this	)
Agreement	
	....
by [ ]	) Director
acting by	)
	)
[a Director and its Secretary *or* by	....
two Directors]	) Secretary/Director

Footnotes

4   **Delete** entirely and **replace** with:

   4   See paras 5.4 and 9.1A–C above and clause 16.3 below.

5   **Delete** entirely and **replace** with:

   5   See paras 5.5–5.10 above. Where there is no guarantor, delete (a) this reference, clauses 14.11.1, 15.6, 16.15.3 and 19, and (b) the references to Guarantor in clauses 15.1.2 and 16.18.

11   **Delete** entirely and **replace** with:

   11   Where there is to be no rent review, amend this definition to 'Rent', and delete clauses 1.6, 4, the first and second bullet points of clause 9.5.1.4 (unless the term is such that there could be a review in an underlease), 16.12 and 19.3.4 and the reference to rent review in clause 10.4.1.6.

19   **Insert** the word 'above' after the words 'see para 11.3'.

20   **Insert** the word 'above' after the words 'see paras 4.10–4.15'.

65   **Delete** entirely and **replace** with:

       65   As to alterations generally, see paras 7.19–7.26 and 7.37A above and clause 10.6.4 below.

66   **Replace** the words 'clause 2' with the words 'clause 6.2'.

67   **Delete** the words 'for reasons that are analogous to those set out in footnote 82 below in relation to ibid, s 19(1)'.

Add   80a   See para 5.13.2 above and Schedule 1 below.

84   **Renumber** footnote 84 as '**80b**' and **insert** after footnote 80a.

Add   80c   See para 7.5A above. This covenant against assignment follows the form recommended by the Report to the ABI Working Party on the Landlord and Tenant (Covenants) Act 1995, referred to at footnote 8 to para 7.5A above.

       80d   Additional possible circumstances and conditions are given in square brackets. They are intended as examples. Not all of them will be appropriate and landlords may wish to add their own additional restrictions. Landlords should give careful consideration to the circumstances and/or conditions which are imposed in the lease, mindful of the effect which they may have on the rent upon review.

       80e   If this circumstance is included, the lease must also include a definition of 'associated company'. If no such provision is included to cover inter-group assignments, the landlord can still rely on the test in clause 9.3.1.1 for protection.

       80f   The landlord should check the terms of any superior lease or mortgage to assess the impact of this condition.

81   **Replace** the words 'defined term' with the words 'defined term to clause 9.1' and **replace** the words 'clause 9.3' with the words 'clause 9.2.3'.

82   **Replace** the words 'an assignment or' with the word 'an'.

83   **Delete** the words 'assignee or'.

89   **Delete** entirely and **replace** with:

       89   See paras 2.22–2.26 above.

90   **Replace** the words 'see para 2.25 above' with the words 'see para 2.24 above'.

93   **Add** to the beginnning of footnote 93 the following:

       See para 8.22A. In the light of *Jervis vHarris* [1995] EGCS 177, CA tenants will wish to resist such clauses or, where that is not possible, try to limit the amount of expenditure which a landlord can recover. The advantages for the landlord of this clause must be weighed against the potential liability that it creates under the Defective Premises Act 1972, s 4(4).

Add: 94a   See para 7.37A above. If the works are being carried out for the tenant then the landlord will not want to accept the liabilities which are placed on a 'client' under the Construction (Design and Management) Regulations 1994 and the Approved Code of Practice published by the Health and Safety Commission. The landlord will need to ensure that the tenant actually makes the declaration required and that it obtains the notification served on the landlord by the Health and Safety Executive.

97   **Delete** entirely and **replace** with:

       97   See clause 16.15.5.

Add: 102a   See paras 9.1A–9.1C above.

Add: 142a   See paras 9.1A–9.1C above. No attempt has been made in this lease to provide for an automatic release of the landlord from the landlord's covenants when he transfers his interest in the property and the landlord will therefore have to follow the procedure laid down in s 6 of the Landlord and Tenant (Covenants)

Act 1995. By clause 10.18 above, however, the tenant covenants not to unreasonably withhold consent to a request for release by the landlord under the 1995 Act, section 8. This will give the landlord a remedy in damages in the event of the tenant's breach. For possible ways of avoiding ongoing liability without contravening the anti-avoidance provisions of the 1995 Act, see para 9.1C, footnote 1 above.

144 **Delete** entirely and **replace** with:

144 As to VAT generally, see paras 2.22–2.26 above.

Add: **152a** See para 5.5 above. The liability of the guarantor should be expressed to last while the tenant or assignee is bound by the tenant's covenants contained in the lease, rather than while the lease is vested in that person, in order to take account of the possibility of an excluded assignment being made and the tenant or assignee remaining liable.

152b See para 5.6.7 above. The Landlord and Tenant (Covenants) Act 1995 is unclear as to whether the liability of a contractual guarantor can be expressed to extend to any period during which the tenant is bound by an authorised guarantee agreement but arguably the policy of the 1995 Act suggests that this should be possible.

162 **Replace** the words 'in clause 19.13.2' with the words 'in clause 13.2'.

Add: **164** See para 5.13.2 and clause 9.3.1 above. The content of an authorised guarantee agreement is prescribed by the 1995 Act, ss 16(4) and (5).

165 The tenant should ensure that he takes an express indemnity from the assignee since the statutory indemnities on assignment of the lease do not apply to new tenancies under the 1995 Act, s 14.

166 This may be outside the scope of an authorised guarantee agreement (see 1995 Act, s 16 (4) (b)). However, in the event of the clause falling foul of s 16 (4) (b) it should be severable from the rest of the agreement.

167 See footnote 160 above.

168 Tenants may wish to insert a provision of this nature as there may be no continuing contact between the tenant and the assignee.

169 Clause 6 is adapted from the College of Law's 'Privity of Contract: A Practitioner's Guide' (1995). The clause is a tenant's amendment, extending to the tenant the benefit of the default notice regime provided for in the 1995 Act which would not otherwise apply. The right of a guarantor to be served with a default notice does not apply whilst the person they are guaranteeing is the current tenant (s 17 (3) of the 1995 Act being concerned only with guarantors of former tenants).

165 **Renumber** footnote 165 as '170'.

FORM 1.2 LEASE OF A WHOLE BUILDING: SHORT FORM

8. Alienation

Add to clause 8.3 the following:

provided that the Landlord shall be entitled (for the purposes of the Landlord and Tenant Act 1927, section 19(1A)) to require as a condition of its consent that the Tenant (here meaning the person in whom the term is vested at the date of the application for assignment) executes and delivers to the Landlord before the completion of the assignment an authorised guarantee agreement in the form that the Landlord reasonably requires

Footnotes

1   **Add:** Particular attention will need to be given to the alienation provisions. Clause 8.3 entitles the landlord to require the outgoing tenant to enter into an authorised guarantee agreement upon assignment. However, with a short-term agreement an absolute bar against assignment may be appropriate. Alternatively the more specific restrictions of Form 1.1, clause 9 may need to be introduced.

FORM 2.1 OFFICES

CONTENTS

Add: 12.18   Consent to Landlord's release
Add: Schedule 1   Authorised guarantee agreement.

1. Definitions and interpretation

Renumber clause 1.20 as '1.20.1' and **add** the following:

1.20.2   "1995 Act" means the Landlord and Tenant (Covenants) Act 1995

Replace clause 1.27 with the following:

1.27   "Tenant" means any person bound by the tenant covenants of this Lease from time to time

1.27.1   the person from time to time in whom the tenant's interest under this Lease is vested and

1.27.2   any person in whom the tenant's interest under this Lease had been vested and who has not been released by the 1995 Act

11. Alienation

Replace clauses 11.1–11.9 with the following:

11.1   *Definitions*

In this Lease:

11.1.1   "Application" means an application from the Tenant for the Landlord's consent to the Proposed Assignment

11.1.2   "Authorised Guarantee Agreement" means a deed in the form set out in Schedule 1 with such amendments (if any) as the Landlord reasonably requires and being an authorised guarantee agreement as defined in the 1995 Act, section 16

11.1.3   "Current Tenant" means the person in whom the Term is vested at the date of the Application

11.1.4   "Proposed Assignee" means the person stated in the Application to whom the Current Tenant wishes to assign this Lease

11.1.5 "Proposed Assignment" means a proposed assignment of the Property by the Current Tenant to the Proposed Assignee for which the Landlord's consent is requested in the Application

11.1.6 "Proposed Guarantor" means the person or persons (if any) who must not be or include the Current Tenant stated in the Application who it is proposed will guarantee to the Landlord the obligations of the Proposed Assignee

11.2 *General covenants*

The Tenant covenants with the Landlord:

11.2.1 except to the extent permitted under the subsequent provisions of this clause not to:

- part with possession of the Property or any part of it
- permit another to occupy the Property or any part of it
- share the occupation of the Property or any part of it
- hold the property or any part of it on trust for another

but the Tenant may allow a company that is a member of the same group as the Tenant (within the meaning of the 1954 Act section 42) to occupy the whole or part of the Property for so long as both companies remain members of the same group and otherwise than in a manner that transfers or creates a legal estate

11.2.2 not to assign underlet or charge part only of the property

11.2.3 not to assign the whole of the Property without the consent of the Landlord (such consent not to be unreasonably withheld) provided that the Landlord shall be entitled (for the purposes of section 19(1A) of the Landlord and Tenant Act 1927):

11.2.3.1 to withhold its consent in any of the circumstances set out in clause 11.3.1 and

11.2.3.2 to impose all or any of the matters set out in clause 11.3.2 as a condition of its consent

and the provisos to this clause 11.2.3 shall operate without prejudice to the right of the Landlord to withhold such consent on any other ground or grounds where such withholding of consent would be reasonable or to impose any further condition or conditions upon the grant of consent where the imposition of such consent or consents would be reasonable

11.2.4 not to underlet the whole of the Property without the consent of the landlord such consent not to be unreasonably withheld where the Tenant has complied with the provisions of clause 11.5

11.2.5 not to charge the whole of the Property without the consent of the Landlord such consent not to be unreasonably withheld

11.3 *Circumstances and conditions*

11.3.1 The circumstances referred to in clause 11.2.3.1 are:

11.3.1.1 Where in the reasonable opinion of the Landlord the Proposed Assignee is not of sufficient financial standing to enable it to comply with the Tenant's covenants and conditions contained in this Lease throughout the Term

[11.3.1.2 Where the Proposed Assignee is an associated company of the Current Tenant

11.3.1.3 Where in the reasonable opinion of the Landlord the value of the Landlord's interest in the Property would be diminished or otherwise adversely affected by the Proposed Assignment on the assumption (whether or not a fact) that the Landlord wished to sell its interest the day following completion of the Proposed Assignment of this Lease to the Proposed Assignee;

11.3.1.4 Where the Proposed Assignee enjoys diplomatic or state immunity [but this circumstance shall not apply where the Proposed Assignee is the Government of the United Kingdom of Great Britain and Northern Ireland or any department thereof]

11.3.1.5 Where the Proposed Assignee is not resident [in the EC] [in a jurisdiction where reciprocal enforcement of judgments exists]]

11.3.2 The conditions referred to in clause 11.2.3.2 are:

11.3.2.1 The execution and delivery to the Landlord prior to completion of the Proposed Assignment of an Authorised Guarantee Agreement

11.3.2.2 The payment to the Landlord of all rents and other sums which have fallen due under this Lease prior to the date of the Proposed Assignment

[11.3.2.3 The provision of any requisite consent of any superior landlord or mortgagee and confirmation that any lawfully imposed condition of such consent has been satisfied

11.3.2.4 On a Proposed Assignment to a Limited Company the execution and delivery to the Landlord by the Proposed Guarantor prior to the Proposed Assignment of a deed of covenant guaranteeing the performance of the Proposed Assignee [in the form of clauses 21.1–21.3 or] in such [other] form as the Landlord reasonably requires

11.3.2.5 The execution and delivery to the Landlord prior to the Proposed Assignment of a rent deposit deed for such sum as the Landlord may reasonably determine in such form as the Landlord may reasonably require together with the payment by way of cleared funds of the sum specified in the rent deposit deed

11.3.2.6 The application is accompanied by:

- certified copies of the Proposed Assignee's or Proposed Guarantor's audited accounts for each of the three financial years immediately preceding the date of the Application
- references from:
- the Proposed Assignee's or Proposed Guarantor's bankers confirming that the Proposed Assignee or Proposed Guarantor is considered good for the rent payable under this Lease and

- if the Proposed Assignee or Proposed Guarantor is a lessee of other premises at least one of its lessors confirming that the Proposed Assignee or Proposed Guarantor has been a satisfactory lessee and
[• an undertaking from Solicitors acting for the Current Tenant or for the Proposed Assignee or Proposed Guarantor to pay all costs disbursements and any VAT thereon which may be properly incurred by the Landlord in considering the Application whether or not consent is granted and in granting consent (if it is granted)]]

11.3.2.7 If at any time prior to the Proposed Assignment taking place the circumstances (or any of them) specified in clause 11.3.1 apply the Landlord may revoke its consent to the Proposed Assignment by written notice to the tenant

11.4 *Determinations*

11.4.1 Any question of whether or not any of the circumstances set out in clause 11.3.1 apply in relation to the Proposed Assignment or as to whether any of the conditions referred to in clause 11.3.2 should be imposed shall be determined by the Landlord and if the Landlord determines that any of the circumstances apply or that any of the conditions should be imposed the Landlord must give written notice to that effect to the Tenant and such notification will be binding on the Tenant unless within 14 days of the service of the notice the Tenant serves on the Landlord a counternotice ("Counternotice") requiring the Landlord's determination to be reviewed by a third party in accordance with clause 11.4.2

11.4.2 If a Counternotice is served the Landlord's determination shall be reviewed by an independent third party acting as an expert and not as an arbitrator who shall be agreed or appointed in accordance with clause 11.4.3 and whose decision shall be conclusive and binding

11.4.3 The third party must be a Chartered Surveyor with not less than 10 years' post qualification experience appointed by agreement between the Landlord and the Tenant or in the absence of such agreement nominated at the request of either of them by the President for the time being of The Royal Institution of Chartered Surveyors (or his duly appointed deputy or anyone authorised by him to make appointments on his behalf)

11.4.4 The fees payable to the President or any such third party shall be borne and paid by the Landlord and the Tenant in such shares and in such manner as the third party shall determine and failing any such decision in equal shares (and if one party shall pay all the fees it shall be entitled to recover from the other any appropriate share which is due)

11.5 *Underletting*

11.5.1 Any consent of the Landlord to an underletting of the whole of the Property will be subject to conditions that:

11.5.1.1 the undertenant enters into a deed with the Landlord in which the undertenant covenants that during the period when the undertenant is bound by the tenant covenants contained in the underlease together with any additional period during which the undertenant is bound by an authorised guarantee agreement the undertenant observe and perform the provisions of this Lease (excluding the covenant as to the payment of rent) and the provisions of the underlease

11.5.1.2 the underlease is granted without a fine or premium at a rent no lower than the then open market rent approved by the Landlord (such approval not to be unreasonably withheld)

11.5.1.3 the rent is payable in advance on the same days as rent is payable under this Lease

11.5.1.4 the underlease contains provisions approved by the Landlord (such approval not to be unreasonably withheld):

- for the upwards-only review of the rent on the basis set out in clause 6 or in such other form as the Landlord reasonably requires or approves
- for the rent to be reviewed either on the Review Dates or on such other dates approved by the Landlord by which the rent is reviewed no less frequently
- prohibiting the undertenant from doing or allowing any act or thing in relation to the Property inconsistent with or in breach of the provisions of this lease
- for re-entry by the underlandlord on breach of any covenant by the undertenant
- imposing an absolute prohibition against all dealings with the Property other than an assignment or charge of the whole
- prohibiting any assignment of the whole of the Property without the consent of the Landlord under this Lease and except on the basis set out in clauses 11.1–11.5 of this Lease such provisions being incorporated into the underlease
- prohibiting any charge of the whole of the Property without the consent of the Landlord under this Lease
- prohibiting the undertenant from parting with possession or permitting another to share or occupy or hold on trust for another the Property or any part of it
- imposing in relation to any permitted assignment the same obligations for registration with the Landlord as are in this Lease in relation to dispositions by the Tenant
- excluding the provisions of the 1954 Act, sections 24–28 from the letting created by the underlease

11.5.2 The tenant covenants with the Landlord:

11.5.2.1 to enforce the performance by every undertenant of the provisions of the underlease and not at any time to waive any breach of the covenants or conditions on the part of any undertenant or assignee of any underlease nor (without the consent of the Landlord such consent not to be unreasonably withheld) to vary the terms of any underlease

11.5.2.2 not to agree any reviewed rent with the undertenant without the approval of the Landlord such approval not to be unreasonably withheld

11.5.2.3 not to agree any appointment of a person as a third party determining the revised rent without the approval of the Landlord such approval not to be unreasonably withheld

11.5.2.4 to incorporate as part of its representations to that third party representations required by the Landlord

11.5.2.5 to give the Landlord details of every rent review within twenty-eight days of its outcome

11.5.2.6 not to grant the underlease or permit the undertenant to occupy the Property unless an order has been obtained under the 1954 Act, section 38(4)

11.5.2.7 not to accept the surrender of or forfeit or otherwise determine any underlease without the consent of the Landlord

11.6   *Insolvency of covenantors*

The Tenant covenants with the Landlord:

11.6.1 to give notice to the Landlord within fourteen days if any person who has entered into covenants with the Landlord under the provisions of this clause (where that person has not been released from these obligations) becomes insolvent (as defined in clause 6.2) or dies

11.6.2 if requested by the Landlord following the service of a notice under clause 11.6.1 to procure that within 14 days of the request some other person reasonably acceptable to the Landlord enters into covenants with the Landlord in substantially the same form

11.7   *Notice to the Landlord of alienation*

Within twenty-one days of any assignment charge underlease or any transmission or other devolution relating to the Property the Tenant covenants with the Landlord to produce for registration with the Landlord's solicitor a certified copy of any relevant document and to pay the Landlord's solicitor's reasonable charge for registration of at least £25

12. Tenant's other covenants

Add clause 12.6.4 as follows:

12.6.4   without prejudice to the generality of the above:

12.6.4.1 to comply at the Tenant's expense with the Construction (Design and Management) Regulations 1994 ("CDM Regulations") and to be the only client (as defined in the CDM Regulations) and to fulfil in relation to all and any works all the obligations of the client as set out in or reasonably to be inferred from the CDM Regulations and to make a declaration to that effect to the Health and Safety Executive in accordance with the Approved Code of Practice publicised from time to time by the Health and Safety Commission in relation to the CDM Regulations and the provisions of clause 14.2.9 shall apply to these obligations and

12.6.4.2 at the end of the Term forthwith to deliver to the Landlord any and all health and safety files relating to the Property in accordance with the CDM Regulations

12.8 *Consent to Landlord's release*

Not to unreasonably withhold consent to a request made by the Landlord under the 1995 Act, section 8 for a release from the landlord covenants of this Lease

21. Guarantor

Insert the following immediately after the heading:

21.1 The Guarantor's covenants with the Landlord are as sole or principal debtor or covenantor with the Landlord for the time being and with all of its successors in title (without the need for any express assignment) so that the Guarantor's obligations to the Landlord will last:

21.1.1 while the Tenant is bound by the tenant's covenants under this Lease and

21.1.2 for any period during which the Tenant shall be liable under any Authorised Guarantee Agreement required by the Landlord pursuant to clause 11.3

Renumber clauses 21.1–21.3.2 as 21.2–21.4.2 and **renumber** references to these clauses in the text.

In clause 21.2 (as renumbered) **replace** the words 'The Guarantor . . . in title:' with the words 'The Guarantor covenants:'.

SCHEDULE 1

After the words '[WE CERTIFY . . . gives effect]' **insert** Schedule 1 as follows:

SCHEDULE 1

<u>DATED</u>   199

and

AUTHORISED GUARANTEE AGREEMENT

[address of the Property]

[Name of Landlord's Solicitors]
[Address:

                                                 ]

Tel: [   ]
Fax: [   ]
Ref: [   ]

AUTHORISED GUARANTEE AGREEMENT

DATE: 199

PARTIES:

(1)   [   ] of [
                                      ] ("Landlord") and
(2)   [   ] of [
                                      ] ("Tenant")

1. Definitions and recitals

1.1   This deed is supplemental to a lease [an underlease] ("the Lease") dated the [   ] and made between (1) [the Landlord] and (2) [the Tenant] by which the property known as [   ] ("the Property") was demised for a term of [   ] years from [and including] the [   ] ("the Term") subject to the payment of the rent[s] reserved by and the performance of the provisions of the Lease

1.2 The reversion immediately expectant on the determination of the Term [remains *or* is now] vested in the Landlord and the unexpired residue of the Term [remains *or* is now] vested in the Tenant

1.3 The Lease contains provisions prohibiting the Tenant from assigning the Property without the consent of the Landlord such consent not to be unreasonably withheld in certain circumstances and further provides that any consent will be subject to a condition that the Tenant enters into an authorised guarantee agreement as defined in the Landlord and Tenant (Covenants) Act 1995 ("the 1995 Act")

1.4 The Landlord has agreed (at the request of the Tenant) to grant a licence to the Tenant to assign its estate and interest in the Property to [   ]of [   ] ("Assignee") subject to the Tenant and the Assignee entering into a formal licence in the form required by the Landlord and the Tenant entering into this Authorised Guarantee Agreement.

1.5 All terms defined in the Lease have the same meanings when used in this deed except where the contrary appears

2. Authorised Guarantee Agreement

2.1 This Deed is an authorised agreement as defined in the 1995 Act section 16

2.2 Nothing in this Deed imposes on the Tenant:

- any requirement to guarantee the performance under the Lease of any person other than the Assignee or
- any liability restriction or other requirement (of whatever nature) in relation to any time after the Assignee is released by the Act from its obligations under the Lease

3. Tenant's covenants

The Tenant covenants with the Landlord and (without the need for any express assignment) with all of the successors in title:

3.1 if the Assignee does not pay the Rent or any other sum due under the Lease on the date on which it is due to pay to the Landlord on demand the Rent or other sum

3.2 if the Assignee is in breach of any provision of the Lease to remedy that breach on demand and to indemnify and keep indemnified the Landlord against all Losses suffered by the Landlord as a result (directly or indirectly) of that breach

3.3 in addition to the obligations set out in clauses 3.1 and 3.2 and if the Lease is disclaimed by the Assignee's trustee in bankruptcy or liquidator:

3.3.1 to pay to the Landlord on demand an amount equal to the Rent and other sums of a recurring nature that would have been payable under the Lease for the period beginning on the date of disclaimer and ending on the earliest of:

- the date upon which the Property is re-let
- the expiry of the Term
- the expiry of the period of [one year] beginning on the date of the disclaimer or

3.3.2   if requested by the Landlord within ninety days of disclaimer to take from the Landlord a lease of the Property from the date of disclaimer for the residue of the Term at the Rent payable at the time of disclaimer or (where a rent review is pending at the time of disclaimer at the Rent that is subsequently agreed or determined under clause 6 of the Lease to have been payable at the time of disclaimer) and upon the same terms as those contained in the Lease with all provisions of a periodical nature (including for example those relating to review of the Rent) expressed to apply on the actual dates that would have applied if the Lease had not been disclaimed and

3.3.3   to pay the costs of the Landlord incurred in relation to the disclaimer and where appropriate the grant of the lease to the Tenant

4.   Application of Tenant's covenants

The obligations of the Tenant set out in clause 3 will continue to apply even if:

4.1   the Landlord grants any time or indulgence to the Assignee or fails to enforce payment of the Rent or any other sum or the performance of the terms of the Lease

4.2   the Landlord refuses to accept the Rent tendered when the Landlord was entitled (or would after the service of a notice under the Law of Property Act 1925, section 146 be entitled) to re-enter the Property

4.3   the terms of the Lease are varied except where the variation is a relevant variation as defined in the 1995 Act, section 18(4)

4.4   a revised Rent has been agreed or determined under clause 6 of the Lease [including any stepped rent phased rent or other rental formula that may be agreed]

4.5   the Assignee surrenders part of the Demised Premises and where this happens the Liability of the Tenant under the Lease continues for the part of the Demised Premises not surrendered after making any necessary apportionments under the Law of Property Act 1925, section 140

4.6   the Tenant would have been released by any other event

5.   Duration of the Tenant's covenant

[5.1]   The obligations of the Tenant set out in clause 3 above apply for the period beginning on the date upon which the Property is assigned to the Assignee and ending on the date upon which the Assignee is released by the 1995 Act from its obligations under the Lease

[5.2   The Landlord covenants with the Tenant that it will notify the Tenant in writing within [   ] days of the Assignee being released by the 1995 Act from its obligations under the Lease]

[6.   Recovery of payments

6.1   The Landlord covenants that before attempting to recover any such payment as is described in clause 6.2 from the Tenant it will serve on the Tenant a notice as if that payment was a fixed charge under the 1995 Act

6.2   The payment referred to in clause 6.1 is any amount payable in respect of any breach of covenant by the Assignee which:

6.2.1   has been finally determined by a court or in binding arbitration; or

6.2.2   has been agreed between the Landlord and the Assignee

6.3   The notice in respect of the payments referred to in clause 6.2 shall be in the form prescribed by section 27 of the 1995 Act with such variations as may be appropriate to the circumstances

6.4   The Tenant shall not be liable for any of the payments referred to in clause 6.2 unless within the period of six months of the payment being determined or agreed the Landlord serves on the Tenant a notice under this clause]

SIGNED as a deed (but not   )
delivered until the date of this   )
Agreement)

by [   ]   )   ....
)   Director
acting by   )
)

[a Director and its Secretary *or* by   ....
two Directors]   )   Secretary/Director
Secretary/Director

Footnotes

2   **Delete** entirely and **replace** with:

    2   Where there is no guarantor delete (a) this reference, clauses 1.30.3, 18.6 and 21 and (b) the references to 'Guarantor' in clauses 1.33 and 18.1.2.

3   **Delete** entirely and **replace** with:

    3   Where there is to be no rent review amend this definition to 'Rent' and delete clauses 1.8, 1.26, 6, the first and second bullet points of clause 11.5.1.4 (unless the term is long enough for there to be a review in an underlease) and 21.3.4 and the reference to rent review in clause 12.4.17.

11   **Add** the word 'above' after the words 'see para 11.12'.

12   **Add:** See also note 102a to Form 1.1 above. The question of the landlord's release from its covenants upon a transfer of his interest will be of increased significance where he has covenanted to provide services.

FORM 2.2   SHOP IN A CENTRE

CONTENTS

Add: 12.18   Consent to Landlord's release
Add: Schedule 1   Authorised guarantee agreement.

1. Definitions and interpretation

Renumber clause 1.23 as '1.23.1' and **add:** '1.23.2   "1995 Act" means the Landlord and Tenant (Covenants) Act 1995'.

12. Tenant's other covenants

Delete '12.16–12.17' (*continue as Form 2.1, clauses 12.16–12.17*) and **replace** with '12.16–12.18 (*continue as Form 2.1, clauses 12.16–12.18*).

SCHEDULE 1

After clauses 18–21 **add:**

SCHEDULE 1   (*continue as Form 2.1, Schedule 1*)

FORM 3 LEASE OF A UNIT ON AN ESTATE OR BUSINESS PARK

CONTENTS

Add: 12.18   Consent to Landlord's release
Add: Schedule 1   Authorised guarantee agreement.

1. Definitions and interpretation

Renumber clause 1.21 as '1.21.1' and **add:** '1.21.2 "1995 Act" means the Landlord and Tenant (Covenants) Act 1995'.

12. Tenant's other covenants

Add: 12.6.4   (*continue as Form 2.1, clause 12.6.4*).
Add: 12.18 (*continue as Form 2.1, clause 12.18*)
Delete '17.7–21.3 (*continue as Form 2.1, clause 17.7–21.3*)' and **replace** with '17.7–21.4 (*continue as Form 2.1, clause 17.7–21.4*)'

SCHEDULE 1

After clauses 17.7–21.4 **add:**

SCHEDULE 1   (*continue as Form 2.1, Schedule 1*).

FORM 9 CONTAMINATED LAND: LANDLORD ASSUMES RESPONSIBILITY FOR ANY HISTORIC POLLUTION

0 Historic Pollution

Delete clause 0.1.4 and **replace** with:

0.1.4 "Regulatory Authority" means the Environment Agency a local authority the Health and Safety Executive and any other government department body authority inspectorate or agency (existing or to be formed) responsible for administering or enforcing the law relating to pollution.

Appendix 2

Checklist for tenant's solicitor

A PRELIMINARY

		para
Add:	1 If client inexperienced, consider referring to DoE Code of Practice for general information	1.6A

Renumber items 1–12 as 2–13.

Add:	14 Is the lease an 'old lease' or a new tenancy for the purposes of the 1995 Act?	5.11

Renumber item 13 as '15'.

F GUARANTOR/ORIGINAL TENANT

Delete entirely and **replace** with the following:

1	Had a guarantor for tenant been previously agreed?	5.5
2	Amend to:	
2.1	– limit to period during which lease vested in tenant	5.9.1
2.2	– resist guarantor's liability extending to period period during which tenant liable under any authorised guarantee agreement	5.9.1
2.3	– provide for service with copies of notices etc	5.9.3
2.4	– be informed if tenant late in paying rent	5.9.4
2.5	– require equivalent to default notice	5.9.5
2.6	– participate in rent review	5.9.6
2.7	– provide for assign on default	5.9.7
3	Deed between guarantor and tenant	5.9.8
4	Consider any authorised guarantee agreement tenant will be required to enter into on assignment	5.12

M ALIENATION

Add:	3 Consider circumstances/conditions imposed for purposes of 1927 Act, s 19(1A)	7.5A

Renumber items 3–6 as 4–7.

Para

Q REPAIRING COVENANT

Add 9.6 – resist enter, repair and charge clause (or amend)   8.22A

Renumber item 9.6 as '9.7'.

R LANDLORD'S COVENANTS

Add 1 Try to resist landlord's attempt to provide   9.1C
for automatic release

Renumber items 1–4 as 2–5.

U PROVISOS

In item 1 **add:** '(specify dates)'.

In item 2 **add** a closing bracket after the word 'agreed' and an opening bracket before the words '1954 Act'.

Drafting and Negotiating Commercial Leases